SRA
ART
Connections

Level 3

Authors
Rosalind Ragans, Ph.D., Senior Author

Willis "Bing" Davis   Jane Rhoades Hudak, Ph.D.   Bunyan Morris
Tina Farrell   Gloria McCoy   Nan Yoshida

Contributing Author
Jackie Ellett

ART
SOU
RCE
ARTSOURCE

Education Division
The Music Center of Los Angeles County

SRA

Columbus, OH

The McGraw·Hill Companies

Authors

Senior Author
Dr. Rosalind Ragans, Ph.D.
Associate Professor Emerita
Georgia Southern University

Willis "Bing" Davis
Associate Professor Emeritus
Central State University - Ohio
President & Founder of
SHANGO: The Center for the
Study of African American
Art & Culture

Tina Farrell
Assistant Superintendent
Curriculum and Instruction
Clear Creek Independent
School District,
League City, Texas

Jane Rhoades Hudak, Ph.D.
Professor of Art
Georgia Southern University

Gloria McCoy
Former President
Texas Art Education Association
Spring Branch Independent
School District, Texas

Bunyan Morris
Art Teacher
Effingham County School
System, Springfield, Georgia

Nan Yoshida
Art Education Consultant
Retired Art Supervisor
Los Angeles Unified
School District
Los Angeles, California

SRAonline.com

Send all inquiries to:
SRA/McGraw-Hill
8787 Orion Place
Columbus, OH 43240-4027

Printed in the United States of America.

ISBN 0-07-601822-9

4 5 6 7 8 9 RRW 10 09 08 07 06 05

The McGraw-Hill Companies

Contributors

Contributing Author
Jackie Ellett, Ed. S.
Elementary Art Teacher
Duncan Creek Elementary School
Hoschton, Georgia

Contributing Writer
Lynda Kerr, NBCT
Ed.D. Candidate, Art Teacher
Henry County, Georgia

Artsource® Music, Dance, Theatre Lessons
Mark Slavkin, Vice President
for Education, The Music Center of
Los Angeles County
Michael Solomon, Managing Director
Music Center Education Division
Melinda Williams, Concept Originator and
Project Director
Susan Cambigue-Tracey, Project Coordinator

and Writer
Madeleine Dahm, Movement and Dance
Connection Writer
Keith Wyffels, Staff Assistance
Maureen Erbe, Logo Design

More about Aesthetics
Richard W. Burrows
Executive Director, Institute for Arts
Education
San Diego, California

Safe Use of Art Materials
Mary Ann Boykin
Director, The Art School for Children and
Young Adults
University of Houston—Clear Lake
Houston, Texas

Museum Education
Marilyn J. S. Goodman
Director of Education
Solomon R. Guggenheim Museum
New York, New York

Resources for Students with Disabilities
Mandy Yeager
Ph.D. Candidate
The University of North Texas
Denton, Texas

Music Connections
Kathy Mitchell
Music Teacher
Eagan, Minnesota

Student Activities

Cassie Appleby
Glen Oaks Elementary School
McKinney, Texas

Maureen Banks
Kester Magnet School
Van Nuys, California

Christina Barnes
Webb Bridge Middle School
Alpharetta, Georgia

Beth Benning
Willis Jepson Middle School
Vacaville, California

Chad Buice
Craig Elementary School
Snellville, Georgia

Beverly Broughton
Gwinn Oaks Elementary School
Snellville, Georgia

Missy Burgess
Jefferson Elementary School
Jefferson, Georgia

Marcy Cincotta-Smith
Benefield Elementary School
Lawrenceville, Georgia

Joanne Cox
Kittredge Magnet School
Atlanta, Georgia

Carolyn Y. Craine
McCracken County Schools
Paducah, Kentucky

Jackie Ellett
Duncan Creek Elementary School
Hoschton, Georgia

Tracie Flynn
Home School
Rushville, Indiana

Phyllis Glenn
Malcom Bridge Elementary
Bogart, Georgia

Dallas Gillespie
Dacula Middle School
Dacula, Georgia

Dr. Donald Gruber
Clinton Junior High School
Clinton, Illinois

Karen Heid
Rock Springs Elementary School
Lawrenceville, Georgia

Alisa Hyde
Southwest Elementary
Savannah, Georgia

Kie Johnson
Oconee Primary School
Watkinsville, Georgia

Sallie Keith, NBCT
West Side Magnet School
LaGrange, Georgia

Letha Kelly
Grayson Elementary School
Grayson, Georgia

Diana Kimura
Amestoy Elementary School
Gardena, California

Desiree LaOrange
Barkley Elementary School
Fort Campbell, Kentucky

Deborah Lackey-Wilson
Roswell North Elementary
Roswell, Georgia

Dawn Laird
Goforth Elementary School
Clear Creek, Texas

Mary Lazzari
Timothy Road Elementary School
Athens, Georgia

Michelle Leonard
Webb Bridge Middle School
Alpharetta, Georgia

Lynn Ludlam
Spring Branch ISD
Houston, Texas

Mark Mitchell
Fort Daniel Elementary School
Dacula, Georgia

Martha Moore
Freeman's Mill Elementary School
Dacula, Georgia

Connie Niedenthal
Rushville Elementary
Rushville, Indiana

Barbara Patisaul
Oconee County Elementary
School
Watkinsville, Georgia

Elizabeth Paulos-Krasle
Social Circle Elementary
Social Circle, Georgia

Jane Pinneau
Rocky Branch Elementary School
Watkinsville, Georgia

Marilyn Polin
Cutler Ridge Middle School
Miami, Florida

Michael Ramsey
Graves County Schools
Mayfield, Kentucky

Rosemarie Sells
Social Circle Elementary
Social Circle, Georgia

Jean Neelen–Siegel
Baldwin School
Alhambra, California

Debra Smith
McIntosh County School System
Darien, Georgia

Patricia Spencer
Harmony Elementary School
Buford, Georgia

Melanie Stokes
Smiley Elementary School
Ludowici, Georgia

Rosanne Stutts
Davidson Fine Arts School
Augusta, Georgia

Fran Sullivan
South Jackson Elementary School
Athens, Georgia

Kathy Valentine
Home School
Burkburnett, Texas

Debi West
Rock Springs Elementary School
Lawrenceville, Georgia

Sherry White
Bauerschlag Elementary School
League City, Texas

Patricia Wiesen
Cutler Ridge Middle School
Miami, Florida

Deayna Woodruff
Loveland Middle School
Loveland, Ohio

Gil Young
El Rodeo School
Beverly Hills, California

Larry A. Young
Dacula Elementary School
Dacula, Georgia

Table of Contents

What Is Art?

About Art

◀ **Pablo Picasso.**
Mother and Child.

Unit **1** Line and Shape

◀ **Edgar Degas.**
*Little Dancer,
Aged Fourteen.*

Unit 2 Space and Form

◀ **Diego Rivera.**
Kneeling Child on Yellow Background.

Unit 3 Color and Value

▲ **Audrey Flack.**
Strawberry Tart Supreme.

Unit 4 Texture and Balance

◀ **John James Audubon.**
Great Blue Heron.

Unit 5 Pattern, Rhythm, and Movement

9

◀ **Fredric Remington.**
Mountain Man.

Unit 6 Harmony, Variety, Emphasis, and Unity

10

Technique Tips

Activity Tips

What Is Art?

Art is . . .

Painting is color applied to a flat surface.

▲ **Edward Hopper.** (American). *Early Sunday Morning.* 1930.
....
Oil on canvas. $35\frac{3}{16} \times 60\frac{1}{4}$ inches (89.4 × 153 cm.). Whitney Museum of American Art, New York, New York.

Drawing is the process of making art with lines.

▲ **Pablo Picasso.** (Spanish). *Mother and Child.* 1922.
....
Oil on canvas. 40 × 32 inches (100 × 81 cm.). The Baltimore Museum of Art, Baltimore, Maryland.

Sculpture is art that fills up space.

▲ **Kiawak Ashoona.** (Inuit). *Seal Hunter.*
....
Serpentine. Home and Away Gallery, Kennebunkport, Maine.

Architecture is the art of designing and constructing buildings.

▲ **Artist Unknown.** (Roman), *Maison Carée.* 1st century B.C.
....
Nîmes, France.

Printmaking is the process of transferring an original image from one prepared surface to another.

◄ **Maria Sibylla Merian.** (German). *Plate 2 (from "Dissertation in Insect Generations and Metamorphosis in Surinam").* 1719.

Hand-colored engraving on paper. 18 × 13¾ inches (45.72 × 34.93 cm.). National Museum of Women in the Arts, Washington, D.C.

Photography is a technique of capturing an image of light on film.

▲ **Ansel Adams.** (American). *Early Sunday Morning, Merced River, Yosemite Valley, CA.* c. 1950, printed c. 1978.

9⅝ × 12⅞ inches (24.45 × 32.70 cm.). Museum of Modern Art, New York, New York.

Pottery is an object made from clay.

▲ **Artist Unknown.** (China). *Covered Jar.* 1522–1566.

Porcelain painted with underglaze cobalt blue and overglaze enamels. 18½ inches high, 15¾ inches in diameter. (7 cm. high, 6 cm. in diameter). Asia Society of New York, New York.

A mask is a covering for the face to be used in ceremonies and other events.

◄ **Artist Unknown.** (Ivory Coast). *Senufo Face Mask.* Nineteenth to twentieth century.

Wood, horn, fiber, cloth, feather, metal. 14½ inches tall (35.56 cm.). The Metropolitan Museum of Art, New York, New York.

Art is made by people

▶ to communicate ideas.

▶ to express feelings.

▶ to give us well-designed objects.

What Is Art?

Every work of art has three parts.

Subject

The subject is the object you can recognize in the artwork. If a work has no objects, the elements of art are the subject.

Composition

The composition is how the elements and principles are organized in the artwork.

Content

The content is the message or meaning of the artwork. When the work of art is functional, then the function of the work is the meaning.

▶ In which work of art do you think the subject matter is very important?

▶ In which artwork do you think composition is most important?

▶ Which work seems to have the strongest message? Explain.

▶ Which artwork's meaning relates to its function?

▲ **Lorenzo Scott.** (American). *Ballet Dancers.*

Oil on canvas. 50 × 30 inches (127 × 76.2 cm.). Collection of Ann and Ted Oliver.

◀ **Joseph Stella.** (American). *The Voice of the City of New York Interpreted/ The Great White Way Leaving the Subway (White Way I).* c. 1920–22.

Oil and tempera on canvas. $88\frac{1}{2}$ × 54 inches (224.79 × 137.16 cm.). The Newark Museum, Newark, New Jersey.

▲ **Henry Moore.** (British). *Family Group.* 1948–1949.

Bronze (cast 1950), $59\frac{1}{4}$ × $46\frac{1}{2}$ × $29\frac{7}{8}$ inches (150.5 × 118.1 × 75.88 cm.). Museum of Modern Art, New York, New York.

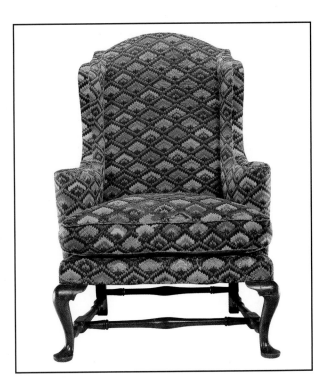

▲ **Caleb Gardner.** (American). *Easy Chair.* 1758.

Walnut, maple, and hand stitched upholstery. $46\frac{3}{8}$ × $32\frac{3}{8}$ × $25\frac{7}{8}$ inches (117.8 × 82.2 × 65.7 cm.). The Metropolitan Museum of Art, New York, New York.

What Is Art?

Subject Matter

Artists make art about many subjects. *Subject matter* is the content of an artist's work. For example, the subject of a painting can be a vase of flowers or a self-portrait. This subject matter is easy to see. The subject matter is harder to understand when the artwork stands for something beyond itself. Look at the artwork on these pages. Notice the different kinds of subject matter.

Still Life

▲ **Paul Cézanne.** (French). *Still Life with Apples. 1895–1898.*
....
Oil on canvas. 27 × 36½ inches (68.58 × 92.71 cm.). The Museum of Modern Art, New York, New York.

Landscape

▲ **Claude Monet.** (French). *Japanese Bridge over a Pool of Water Lilies.* 1899.

Oil on canvas. $36\frac{1}{2} \times 29$ inches (93 × 74 cm.). The Metropolitan Museum of Art, New York, New York.

What Is Art?

Genre

▲ **Jacob Lawrence.** (American). *Street Scene (Boy with Kite).* 1962.

Egg tempera on hardboard. $23\frac{7}{8}$ × 30 inches (60.64 × 76.2 cm.). Conservation Center of the Institute of Fine Arts, New York, New York.

Nonobjective

▲ **Joseph Stella.** (American). *The Voice of the City of New York Interpreted/The Great White Way Leaving the Subway (White Way I).* c. 1920–22.

Oil and tempera on canvas. $88\frac{1}{2} \times 54$ inches (224.79 × 137.16 cm.). The Newark Museum, Newark, New Jersey.

What Is Art?

Portrait

▲ **Diego Rivera.** (Mexican). *Kneeling Child on Yellow Background.* 1927.
Oil on canvas. $25\frac{1}{2} \times 21$ inches (65 × 53 cm.). San Francisco Museum of Modern Art, San Francisco, California.

A Story Shown as Symbols

▲ **Artist Unknown.** (English). *The Five Senses: Hearing. (Detail.)* c. 1650–1675.

White satin embroidered in petit point and enriched with seed pearls and coral. The Metropolitan Museum of Art, New York.

Elements of Art

Art is a language. The words of the language are the elements of art.

Line

Shape

Form

Space

Color

Value

Texture

Principles of Art

Artists organize these words using the principles of art.

Pattern

Rhythm

Balance

Emphasis

Harmony

Variety

Unity

About Art

▲ **Horace Pippin.** (American). *Victorian Parlor II.*
1945. Oil on canvas. $25\frac{1}{4} \times 30$ inches (64.1 × 76.2 cm.). The Metropolitan Museum of Art, New York.

Art History and Culture

Look at the artwork.

▶ What people or objects do you see?

▶ Do they look like people and objects you see around you today? Explain.

Look at the caption.

▶ When was the artwork created?

▶ What can you learn about the artist?

Learn more.

▶ Do some research to find out more about the artist, the artwork, and the time period.

About Art

▲ **Horace Pippin.** (American). *Victorian Parlor II.* 1945.

Oil on canvas. $25\frac{1}{4} \times 30$ inches (64.1 × 76.2 cm.). The Metropolitan Museum of Art, New York.

Look

▶ Look at the work of art. What sounds and smells are in this work of art?

▶ What happened just before and just after in this work of art?

Look Inside

▶ Describe the rest of this house. What is in each room?

▶ Tell or write a story about this work of art with a beginning, a middle, and an end.

▶ How would it feel to sit in one of those chairs?

Look Outside

▶ How is this like or different from your own life?

▶ What does the artist want you to know or think about in this work of art?

▶ What will you remember about this work?

About Art

▲ **Horace Pippin.** (American). *Victorian Parlor II.* 1945.
....
Oil on canvas. $25\frac{1}{4} \times 30$ inches (64.1 $\times$ 76.2 cm.). The Metropolitan Museum of Art, New York.

Art Criticism

Describe

▶ List everything you see in this painting.

Analyze

▶ How has the artist used line, shape, color, value, space, and texture?

▶ How has the artist used rhythm, balance, and variety to organize this painting?

Interpret

▶ What is the artist telling you about the people who live in this room?

Decide

▶ Have you ever seen another artwork like this?

▶ Is it successful because it is realistic?

▶ Is it successful because it is well-organized?

▶ Is it successful because you have strong feelings when you study it?

About Art

▲ **Horace Pippin.** (American). *Victorian Parlor II.* 1945.

Oil on canvas. $25\frac{1}{4} \times 30$ inches (64.1 × 76.2 cm.). The Metropolitan Museum of Art, New York.

How does an artist create art? You can follow the same steps to create your own art.

1. Get an idea.
▶ Inspiration comes from many places. Look around you.

2. Plan your work.
▶ Decide what media you want to use. What materials will you need?

3. Make a sketch.
▶ Think about how you want your artwork to look. Sketch several ideas. Then choose the best idea.

4. Use the media.
▶ Make an artwork based on your best idea. You can practice using the materials first.

5. Share your final work.

Safety

▶ Use art materials only on your artwork.

▶ Keep art materials out of your mouth, eyes and ears.

▶ Use scissors carefully. Keep your fingers away from the blades.

▶ Wash your hands after using the art materials.

▶ Wear an art shirt or smock to protect your clothes.

▶ Use only art materials with a "nontoxic" label.

▶ Keep fingers clear when using a stapler.

▶ Be careful not to breathe chalk or clay dust.

▶ Return art materials to their proper storage place.

▶ Always follow your teacher's directions when using art materials.

Line and Shape

◀ **Pablo Picasso.**
(Spanish). *Mother and Child.* 1922.
Oil on canvas. 40 × 32 inches (100 × 81 cm.). The Baltimore Museum of Art, Baltimore, Maryland.

Artists use line and shape to create all types of art.

In this artwork, Picasso used simple lines and shapes to show the feelings between a mother and child.

Artists use a variety of **lines** to outline objects and show details.

▶ Which lines outline the objects in *Mother and Child*?

▶ How do lines show detail in the mother's hair? Where else do you see lines that show detail?

Artists also use **geometric shapes** and **free-form** shapes.

▶ What main shape did Picasso use to draw the mother and child? What kind of shapes are the leaves?

▶ What complex geometric shapes did Picasso use for the child's right foot?

In This Unit you will learn to use different kinds of lines. You will study:
▶ Kinds of Lines
▶ Line Variations
▶ Geometric and Free-Form Shapes

Pablo Picasso
(1881–1973)

Pablo Picasso was born in Malaga, Spain. One day his father came home to a surprise—his son had finished a portrait. After examining the work, Picasso's father gave his art supplies to the boy. The work was so magnificent, the father vowed to never paint again himself. Picasso was eight.

Picasso went to Paris in 1904 and met many artists and writers. He became a creative leader. He was a painter, a sculptor, a printmaker, and a ceramacist. Picasso is most famous for developing the style of cubism.

Expressive Lines

◀ **Claude Monet.** (French).
*Japanese Bridge over a Pool of
Water Lilies.* 1899.
....
Oil on canvas. 36 $\frac{1}{2}$ × 29 inches (93 × 74
cm.). Metropolitan Museum of Art, New
York, New York.

Look at the landscape paintings on these pages.
Both artists used lines to express different kinds of
weather. Compare the moods of the two paintings.

 Art History and Culture

How did the two artists show different moods in nature?
How did they use lines to express a mood?

▲ **Arthur Lismer.** (Canadian).
September Gale, Georgian Bay.
1921.

Oil on canvas. 48 × 64 $\frac{1}{4}$ inches (122 × 163 cm.). National Gallery of Canada, Ottawa, Ontario, Canada.

Study both landscape paintings.

▶ Find the vertical lines.

▶ Find the horizontal lines.

▶ Identify the diagonal lines.

▶ Where are the curved lines in each painting?

▶ Find the lines that zigzag.

Aesthetic Perception

Seeing Like an Artist Look outside your classroom windows. Look for things such as trees, leaves, and grass. Find lines similar to those in the landscape paintings.

Using Lines

Lines are marks drawn by a tool such as a pencil, pen, or paintbrush as it moves across a surface. There are five different kinds of lines. Each one can make you feel a certain way.

  Vertical lines move straight up and down. They make things look tall, steady, and calm.

 Horizontal lines move straight across from side to side. They give a feeling of calm peace.

Diagonal lines are slanted. They look as if they are falling or rising. They make things look active.

 Zigzag lines are diagonal lines that connect. They give a feeling of excitement.

 Curved lines bend and change direction slowly. They give a feeling of graceful movement.

Practice

Use different kinds of lines to create a weather chart. Use white paper and markers.

1. Fold a sheet of paper into six equal boxes. Each box will show a different weather condition that occurs in nature, such as strong wind, rainstorm, or blizzard. Write the name of one of the weather conditions at the bottom of each box.

2. Use different kinds of lines like the ones above to draw the weather condition written at the bottom of each box.

◀ **Anna Boynton.**
Age 8.

Think about the mood this student artist created
in her weather scene.

Creative Expression

How do different kinds of weather make
you feel? Draw a weather scene that
causes you to have a certain feeling.

1. Think about the different kinds of
   weather where you live. What mood
   does each create?

2. Select the type of weather condition
   you would like to draw. Make a rough
   sketch to plan the scene. Experiment
   with different kinds of lines. Decide
   which lines will best express the mood
   you wish to create.

3. Draw your scene. Be sure to use the
   right kinds of lines to create a calm or
   active feeling.

Art Criticism

Describe List the different
kinds of lines you used in
your scene.

Analyze Did you create a
calm or an active scene? Did
you use lines to express this
feeling?

Interpret If you were to
change the lines, how would
the mood or feeling change?

Decide If you could draw this
scene again, how would you
change it?

Line Variations

Look at the artwork on these pages. Both artists used lines; however, the two pieces of art are very different. Kandinsky used lines as part of the subject, and Borofsky used lines to create a giant face.

▲ **Wassily Kandinsky.**
(Russian). *Improvisation No. 27.* 1912.

Oil paint. 47 $\frac{3}{8}$ × 55 $\frac{1}{4}$ inches (120 × 140.34 cm.). Metropolitan Museum of Art, New York, New York.

 Art History and Culture

Both artists used a variety of lines. What is the difference between the two works of art?

◀ **Jonathon Borofsky.**
(American). *Self Portrait with Big Ears Learning to Be Free.*
....
Latex on wall. Modern Art Museum of Fort Worth, Fort Worth, Texas.

Study both works of art to find a variety of lines.

▶ Find lines that are long and lines that are short.

▶ Find lines that are thick and lines that are thin.

▶ Do you see any lines that look rough? Where are they? Find the lines that look smooth.

▶ Where do you see lines that move in different directions?

Aesthetic Perception

Seeing Like an Artist Look around your classroom. Find lines like those you saw in the paintings.

Using a Variety of Lines

Artists can change lines in many ways to make them look different. You saw **line variety** in *Improvisation No. 27* and *Self Portrait with Big Ears*.

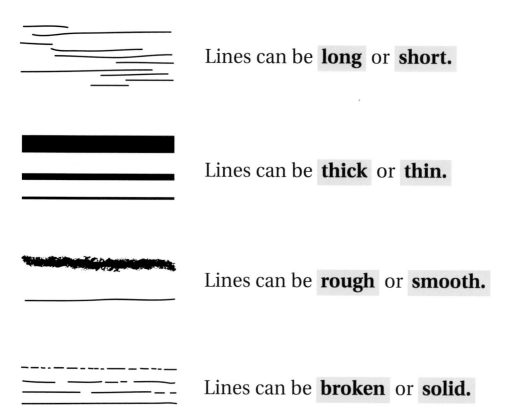

Lines can be **long** or **short.**

Lines can be **thick** or **thin.**

Lines can be **rough** or **smooth.**

Lines can be **broken** or **solid.**

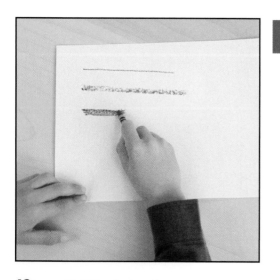

Practice

1. Draw a variety of lines. Use white paper and crayons.

2. Use crayons to make as many different kinds of lines as you can on a sheet of paper.

3. Now use your crayon in different ways to make rough, smooth, thick, and thin lines.

Think about the types of lines this student used to decorate a room.

Creative Expression

What kind of a face would you use to decorate a room? Draw a room and then draw a face on it.

1. Think about a room you would like to decorate. Is it your classroom, your bedroom, or some other room?

2. Draw the room showing the floor, walls, and furniture inside a shoebox.

3. Make some sketches of the kind of face that you would like to see in that room. Select your favorite idea.

4. Using a variety of lines, draw the face in your picture of the room. Use black markers to complete the drawing.

Art Criticism

Describe Describe the room you decided to decorate.

Analyze List the different kinds of lines you used in your painting.

Interpret How did the face you chose to paint affect the mood of the room?

Decide Did you successfully use a variety of lines to paint the face in the picture of your room?

▲ **Janet Fish.** (American).
Yellow Pad. 1997.

Oil on canvas. 36 × 90 inches
(91 × 229 cm.). Columbus Museum,
Columbus, Georgia.

Look at the paintings on these pages. Both artists used lines to create various shapes in their paintings.

 Art History and Culture

Do the paintings appear to be the same style?

Study both still-life paintings to find the following shapes.

▶ Find as many round shapes as you can.

▶ Find the square shapes.

▶ Where are the triangles?

▶ Are there any oval shapes? Where?

▶ Locate the free-form shapes.

Aesthetic Perception

Seeing Like an Artist Think about different shapes or look outside to find them in your environment.

Using Shapes

Everything has a **shape.** Shapes are flat, two-dimensional areas that are geometric or free-form.

Here are some simple **geometric** shapes.

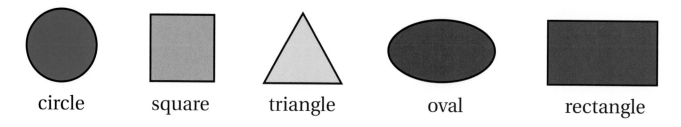

circle   square   triangle   oval   rectangle

Free-form shapes are uneven and irregular. They can look many different ways.

Lines can be used to outline all these shapes.

Practice

Outline geometric and free-form shapes.

1. Find three geometric and three free-form shapes in your classroom.

2. In the air, use your index finger to trace the outline of each object. Close one eye as you trace. Now trace the outside edge of a shape on paper, using a crayon or pencil.

Think about the shapes you see in this student artist's still life.

Creative Expression

What are some of the shapes you see in the objects around you? Paint a still-life picture using lines to make shapes.

1. Arrange five objects of different shapes and sizes in a variety of ways. Select the best arrangement.

2. Which object captures your attention most? Outline the shape of that object on your paper. In the same way, add the shapes of the other objects.

3. Begin to fill your shapes with different colors. Use one color at a time in several places on your picture. Continue to do this until your paper is filled with color.

Art Criticism

Describe What objects did you use in your still life?

Analyze What geometric shapes did you use in your painting? What free-form shapes did you use?

Interpret Give your still life an expressive title.

Decide If you could paint this scene again, what would you do differently?

Complex Geometric Shapes

Look at the artwork on these pages. *Double Saddlebag* was created in North America by a member of the Sioux in 1875. *Mihrab* (the focal area in an Islamic house of worship) was created in Iran about 500 years earlier and is decorated with colorful tiles. Both pieces are decorated with complex geometric shapes.

◀ **Artist unknown.** (Native American, Sioux). ***Double Saddlebag.*** 1875.

Buckskin, canvas, glass beads, sinew, and wool. 45 × 13 inches (113.7 × 33 cm.). Detroit Institute of Arts, Detroit, Michigan.

 Art History and Culture

These works were created by artists from different cultures. Why do you think they used similar shapes?

▲ **Artist unknown.** (Iran). *Mihrab.* 1354.

Faience mosaic of glazed terra cotta cut and embedded in plaster. 11 feet 3 inches × 7 feet 6 inches (3.4 × 2.3 meters). Metropolitan Museum of Art, New York, New York.

Study both works of art and find complex geometric shapes.

▶ Find the shapes that have six sides.

▶ Point to the large diamond shapes in *Double Saddlebag.* Look closely to find smaller diamond shapes in *Mihrab.*

▶ Where do you see some star shapes?

▶ Look at the large shapes in *Double Saddlebag.* What simple geometric shapes are used to make them?

Aesthetic Perception

Design Awareness Notice the shapes of things you see every day, such as the buildings in your neighborhood. What shapes do you see in the spaces around them?

Using Complex Geometric Shapes

Complex geometric shapes are made by combining simple geometric shapes such as triangles, squares, and rectangles. You found examples of complex geometric shapes in the two pieces of art.

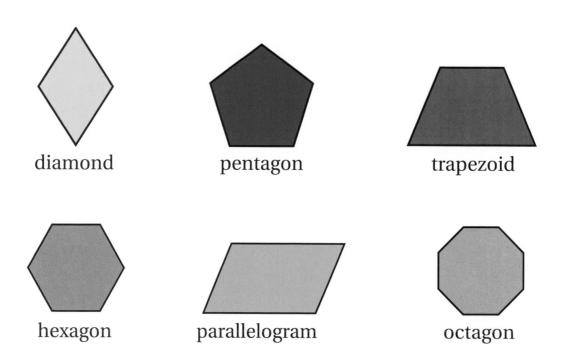

diamond   pentagon   trapezoid

hexagon   parallelogram   octagon

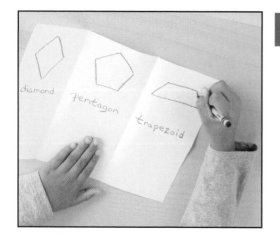

Practice

Use a pencil to draw complex geometric shapes.

1. Fold a sheet of paper into six equal boxes. Print the name of a complex geometric shape at the bottom of each box.

2. Draw one complex geometric shape in each box.

Think about the geometric shapes in this student artist's design.

◀ **Julian Anguiano.**
Age 8.

 🎨 **Creative Expression**

How can you use geometric shapes to create a design? Make your design by using complex geometric shapes.

1. Imagine a design you can create with complex geometric shapes.

2. Use your imagination to make a design using simple and complex geometric shapes.

3. Use your scrap paper to design a frame or border for your art.

 **Art Criticism**

Describe Describe the design you created.

Analyze Name the simple and complex geometric shapes you used.

Interpret Give your design a name.

Decide If you could create this design again, what would you do differently?

Shapes in Architecture

Look at the artwork on these pages. Both works of art show geometric shapes being used for windows and other objects on the building.

▲ **Edward Hopper.**
(American). *The City.*
1927.

Oil on canvas. 28 × 36 inches
(71 × 91 cm.). University of
Arizona Museum of Art, Tucson,
Arizona.

 Art History and Culture

Do the buildings in the paintings appear to be created during the same time period?

Study both pieces of artwork to find the following shapes.

▶ Point to all the square shapes you see.

▶ Where are the rectangles?

▶ Find the triangles.

▶ Do you see any circles?

▶ Find some free-form shapes.

▲ **Giovanni Antonio Canal.** (Italian). *The Clock Tower in the Piazza San Marco.* c. 1730.

Oil on canvas. $20\frac{1}{2} \times 27\frac{3}{8}$ inches (52×71 cm.). Nelson Atkins Museum, Kansas City, Missouri.

Aesthetic Perception

Design Awareness Go outside your classroom and look at the buildings in the neighborhood. Look for geometric and free-form shapes.

Shapes in Architecture

Architecture is the art of designing and planning buildings. You saw examples of architecture in the artwork on the previous pages. An **architect** is the person who plans and designs buildings. Architects use **geometric** and **free-form shapes** in their designs.

Practice

Use a pencil to illustrate geometric and free-form shapes in architecture.

1. On a sheet of paper, use your pencil to draw a building using various shapes.

2. Use your imagination to add smaller geometric and free-form shapes to create the roof, windows, and doors.

◀ **Edwin Vasquez.**
Age 8.

Think about the parts of this student's drawing that have free-form shapes and geometric shapes.

 **Creative Expression**

In the world around you, what kinds of buildings are designed with geometric and free-form shapes? Draw a building using geometric and free-form shapes.

1. Walk outside and choose an area of your school building that you would like to draw.

2. Point out all the geometric shapes you see. Then look for the free-form shapes.

3. Draw the area of the school building you selected. Make sure you include all the geometric and free-form shapes you see.

Art Criticism

Describe Describe the shapes you used in your drawing.

Analyze Where did you place free-form shapes in your drawing? Why?

Interpret How could you completely change the appearance of the building with different shapes?

Decide Does your drawing look like your school? If not, what needs to be changed to improve your drawing?

Shapes of People

Look at the portraits on these two pages. A portrait is a picture of a person. Allen E. Cole used a camera to take the photograph of Silas Johnson in the 1920s. About 150 years earlier, *The Blue Boy* was painted by Thomas Gainsborough. Both portraits show geometric and free-form shapes.

▲ **Allen E. Cole.** (American).
Silas Johnson. 1920.
. . . .
Western Reserve Historical Society,
Cleveland, Ohio.

 Art History and Culture

Why do you think Thomas Gainsborough didn't take a photograph of his subject?

Study both portraits to find geometric and free-form shapes.

▶ Find the circles.

▶ Point to the rectangles you see.

▶ Are there any triangles?

▶ Find the free-form shapes.

▶ Where are the oval shapes?

◀ **Thomas Gainsborough.**
(English). *Jonathan Buttall: The Blue Boy.* c. 1770.
....
Oil on canvas. 70 $\frac{5}{8}$ × 48 $\frac{3}{4}$ inches (180 × 124 cm.). The Huntington Library, San Marino, California.

Aesthetic Perception

Seeing Like an Artist Look at your face in a mirror or think about the shape of your face. Use your index finger to trace the shape of your face. Name the shapes you traced.

Using Shapes

Shapes are all around us. You have already seen different shapes in the landscape paintings on pages 36 and 37. **Free-form shapes** can be found in nature. Puddles, clouds, and flowers are examples of free-form shapes. People also are free-form shapes.

Geometric shapes are usually found in objects that are made by people. Buildings, furniture, and road signs are some examples of geometric shapes.

Most objects have one primary shape. Some objects are made of many smaller shapes.

Practice

Use a pencil to draw the shapes of an object.

1. Choose an object from your classroom to draw. Find the smaller geometric or free-form shapes in it.

2. On a sheet of paper, draw the object by putting together the smaller shapes you see.

◀ **Carolina Monsure.**
Age 8.

Think about the geometric shapes in this student artist's portrait.

 **Creative Expression**

What are the shapes of the faces of some people you know? Draw a portrait using geometric and free-form shapes.

1. Ask a classmate to be your model. Select some objects from the classroom to use as props. Have your model use these props as they pose for you.

2. Look carefully at your model. Find the geometric and free-form shapes.

3. Use chalk to draw your model and the props. Use lines to create the geometric and free-form shapes you see. Fill the shapes with oil pastels.

Art Criticism

Describe What are you wearing in your portrait? What props did you use?

Analyze Where did you use geometric shapes? Where did you use free-form shapes?

Interpret Give your portrait a title. Then, invite your model to give the portrait a title.

Decide Did your portrait turn out as you had hoped? If you were to re-create your portrait, how would you improve it?

Line and Shape

▲ **Jacob Lawrence.** (American.)
Builders No. 1. 1971.
....
Gouache on paper. 30 × 22 inches (76.2 × 55.9 cm).
Birmingham Museum of Art, Birmingham, Alabama.

Critical Thinking

Describe What do you see?

During this step you will collect information about the subject of the work.

▶ What does the credit line tell you about this painting?

▶ Describe the man and the setting.

Analyze How is this work organized?

Think about how the artist has used the elements and principles of art.

▶ Where do you see vertical, horizontal, and diagonal lines?

▶ Where do you see curves?

▶ Where do you see free-form and geometric shapes?

Interpret What is the artist trying to say?

Use the clues you discovered during your analysis to find the message the artist is trying to show.

▶ Is this a calm picture or a busy picture? How do the lines and shapes affect the look of this work?

▶ Do you think the man likes what he is doing?

Decide What do you think about the work?

Use all the information you have gathered to decide whether this is a successful work of art.

▶ Is this painting successful because it is realistic, because it is well organized, or because it has a strong message? Explain.

Show What You Know

Answer these questions on a separate sheet of paper.

1 Lines that make things look tall and calm are called _____.
 A. curved
 B. vertical
 C. horizontal

2 Lines that cause a feeling of excitement are _____.
 A. zigzag
 B. curvy
 C. squiggly

3 Shapes that are uneven and not regular are called _____.
 A. complex
 B. circles
 C. free-form shapes

4 Shapes that are made by combining simple geometric shapes are called _____.
 A. diamonds
 B. complex geometric shapes
 C. horizontal lines

5 The art of designing and planning buildings is called _____.
 A. art designer
 B. planner
 C. architecture

CAREERS IN ART
Advertisers

Have you ever seen a commercial? Commercials are created by advertisers.

Art Directors develop and design advertising campaigns based on market research. The research tells them at what type of audience to aim their advertisements. Then they apply their creative ideas and imagination to find original ways to execute their advertisements.

Layout Artists create the visual aspects of advertising in magazine and newspaper ads, television commercials, and product packaging. They prepare artwork samples for people who plan advertising campaigns.

▲ **Layout Artist**

Line and Shape

Native Americans observed animals to learn from them. The eagle represents wisdom, strength, and vision. They believe that eagles are messengers between man and the creator. Dancers mime the movements of this creature to honor it. They form different body shapes and create straight, diagonal, and curved lines as they dance.

What to Do Create an original eagle dance.

The "Eagle Dance" is sacred to all Native American tribes. The dances show the life of the eagle. Many tribes believe that the eagle can take messages from humans to the world beyond. Think of these ideas as you create your dance.

1. Study pictures of eagles perched on limbs, soaring, and diving. Make these positions with your body.

2. Make a list of actions done by the eagle. Pick one or two actions and express them with movement. Think about the kinds of lines you are creating.

3. Create a simple dance about the eagle. Select three action words from your list. Dance each action for eight counts. End in either a swooping or perched eagle shape.

4. Perform your dance in a group.

▲ American Indian Dance Theatre.

 **Art Criticism**

Describe Describe the way you made your three eagle shapes.

Analyze Explain how you made your eagle movements show two different actions.

Interpret How does your dance express the strength, wisdom, and vision of the eagle?

Decide How well did you show what an eagle is like? How did you use shape and line in your body?

Space and Form

Artists use space and form to make all kinds of artwork.

Degas was the first to show the realistic form of a young ballet dancer. Look at her face. You can see how she is straining to hold her pose. He was also the first to add real fabric and ribbon to a bronze sculpture.

◀ **Edgar Degas.** (French). *Little Dancer, Aged Fourteen.* 1881.

Wax, bronze, tulle skirt, satin hair ribbon, wood base. 39 inches (99 cm.). The Metropolitan Museum of Art, New York, New York.

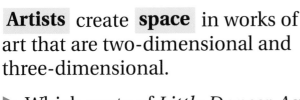

Artists create **space** in works of art that are two-dimensional and three-dimensional.

▶ Which parts of *Little Dancer, Aged Fourteen* are behind or partly covered by other parts?

▶ Describe the area around the sculpture.

Artists create form in three-dimensional work.

▶ Which areas of the sculpture are raised?

▶ Which parts appear to be farther back?

▶ If you walked around to the back of this sculpture, how do you think the girl's head would look on the other side?

In This Unit you will learn about and practice techniques to create the appearance of space on a flat surface. You will also learn about three-dimensional forms. Here are topics you will study:
▶ Space
▶ Depth
▶ Overlapping
▶ Form
▶ Sculpture

Edgar Degas

(1834–1917)
Edgar Degas was born the son of a banker in Paris, France. As a child Degas took drawing lessons and developed his artistic ability. His study of Japanese art led him to experiment with different visual angles. He was best known for his pictures of ballet dancers, café life, and horseracing scenes. His style, subject matter, and ability set him apart from other impressionist artists. Degas was not well known to the public, and his true artistic stature did not become evident until after his death.

Positive and Negative Space

Look at the artwork on these pages. *Sleeveless shirt (two cats)* is an **appliqué,** or decoration made from cutouts. The cotton cloth shapes were sewn onto a woolen background. *Tree of Life* is a paper cutout. Positive and negative spaces bring out the design in both works.

◀ **Artist Unknown.** Coastal Inca (Peru). *Sleeveless Shirt (two cats).* c. 1438–1532.

Wool and cotton. The Metropolitan Museum of Art, Nelson Rockefeller Collection, New York, New York.

 Art History and Culture

Look at these two works of art and how they were created. What do these works tell you about the crafts produced by Incan and Polish people?

Study both works of art to find examples of positive and negative space.

▶ What objects do you see in each work? What colors are they?

▶ What colors are the negative spaces around the objects in each work?

▶ How do the empty spaces in both works of art help make the objects stand out?

◀ **Stanistawa Bakula.** (Polish). *Tree of Life.* 1962.

Cut paper. 12 $\frac{3}{8}$ × 7 $\frac{1}{2}$ inches (31 × 19 cm.). Museum of International Folk Art, Santa Fe, New Mexico.

Aesthetic Perception

Design Awareness Notice how the negative space around clouds changes as the clouds are moved by the wind.

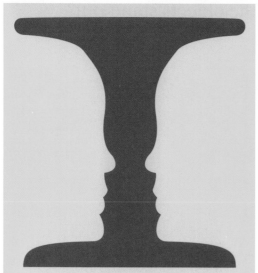

Using Positive and Negative Space

In a work of art, the area that shapes and objects fill is called **positive space.** The empty space is called **negative space.**

Negative space can be just as important as positive space. Negative space affects the way shapes and objects look. What objects do you see in the pictures to the left? Can you tell which areas are positive space and which are negative space?

Practice

Create a design with positive and negative space. Use crayons.

1. Fold a piece of paper into two equal parts. Draw a large free-form shape on the outside of each half.

2. Use crayons to color the negative spaces only.

3. Open the paper. How do the negative spaces help you see the shapes that you drew?

Think about how the student artist created positive and negative space in her print.

◀ **Palmira Caloncit.**
Age 8.

 **Creative Expression**

What shapes do you find interesting? Create a two-dimensional paper mask.

1. Study *Sleeveless Shirt* and *Tree of Life*.

2. Choose a light color, full-size sheet of construction paper. Choose a contrasting color for the half sheet.

3. Lay the half sheet on top of the left side of the full sheet of construction paper.

4. When all pieces are positioned in the correct location, glue them into place.

Art Criticism

Describe List the steps you followed to make your mask.

Analyze Identify the positive and negative space.

Interpret What kind of expression does your mask have?

Decide Does your mask have positive and negative space with both sides mirroring each other?

Creating Depth

Look at the artwork on these pages. Both artists show depth by making the objects in the foreground larger and the objects in the background smaller.

▲ **Artist Unknown.** (United States). *Washington's Headquarters 1780.* c. 1876.

Mixed-media. 21 $\frac{1}{4}$ × 28 inches (54 × 71 cm.). Smithsonian American Art Museum, Washington, D.C.

 Art History and Culture

What time in American History does the painting *Washington's Headquarters* tell about?

▲ **Joseph Mallord William Turner.** (English). *Mortlake Terrace.* 1826.

Oil on canvas. 36 $\frac{1}{4}$ × 48 $\frac{1}{8}$ inches (92 × 122 cm.). National Gallery of Art, Washington, D.C.

Study both paintings to see how the artists create depth by making objects seem near or far away.

► Find the objects that seem to be closest.

► Which objects seem to be farthest away?

► Which objects can you see most clearly?

► Draw a line with your finger between the front and back scenes. Do the objects in the front and the back look like they are the same size?

Aesthetic Perception

Design Awareness What looks smaller, the objects closer to you or the objects farther away?

Creating Depth

Depth in artwork is created when some objects seem to be very close and others seem to be far away.

Just like in real life, objects in artwork that are larger seem to be closer. Objects that are smaller seem to be farther away. Also, objects in artwork that have clear, sharp edges and many details seem closer. Objects that have fuzzy edges and little detail seem farther away.

Foreground is the part of the picture plane that appears closest to the viewer. The foreground is usually at the bottom of the picture plane.

Background is the part of the picture plane that seems to be farthest from the viewer. It is usually located at the top of the picture plane.

Practice

Draw objects in the **foreground** and in the **background.**

1. Near the bottom of your paper, draw a large animal or object.

2. Draw the same animal or object near the top of your paper, but make it much smaller.

◀ **Katie Waters.**
Age 9.

Think about how the student artist showed depth in her drawing.

Creative Expression

What does your favorite outdoor place look like? Draw it using a variety of lines.

1. Think about a place where there are lots of animals.

2. Make a rough sketch of the animals and other objects you want in your scene. Show depth by drawing animals and objects larger in the foreground and smaller in the background.

3. Fill your scene with color.

Art Criticism

Describe Name the animals and objects you put in your picture.

Analyze What did you put in the background?

Interpret What title would you give your drawing?

Decide Were you able to create a feeling of depth in your work?

Look at the landscape paintings on these pages. In *Haitian Landscape,* Joseph-Jean Gilles created a landscape of a farming community by overlapping houses, trees, and gardens. In *The Locust Trees with Maple,* Sylvia Plimack Mangold added a sense of depth by painting branches that cover each other. This makes the trees in front look closer to the viewer.

▲ **Sylvia Plimack Mangold.** (American). *The Locust Trees with Maple.* 1990.

Oil on linen. Brooke Alexander Gallery, New York, New York.

Art History and Culture

Artists paint scenes from the environment where they live.

▲ **Joseph Jean-Gilles.**
(Haitian). *Haitian Landscape.* 1973.

. . . .

Oil on canvas. 30 × 48 inches (76 × 122 cm.). Art Museum of the Americas, Organization of American States, Washington, D.C.

Study both paintings to see how overlapping creates a feeling of depth.

▶ Find objects in each painting that overlap.

▶ Which branches in *The Locust Trees with Maple* look closer to you? Which look farther away?

▶ What objects cover parts of the houses in *Haitian Landscape?* What objects do the houses cover?

▶ Describe the objects in *Haitian Landscape* that look closest to you. Which look farthest away?

Aesthetic Perception

Design Awareness Look out a window and find examples of objects that overlap.

Creating Overlapping

Overlapping occurs when one object covers part of a second object. Overlapping makes the object in front seem closer to the viewer.

When objects overlap, they create depth, or the appearance of distance, on a flat surface. The object in front appears to be closer to the viewer, and the second object seems to be farther away.

Practice

Draw shapes that overlap. Use pencil or crayon.

1. Create a feeling of depth in a design by overlapping geometric shapes.

2. Draw one large shape. Then draw a second shape so that part of it is hidden behind the large shape.

3. Add other shapes.

Think about how the student artist created a sense of depth by overlapping branches.

Creative Expression

How do the trees look when you are walking toward them? Create a drawing of overlapping trees and branches.

1. Think about the different parts of a tree. How do the brances look? Sketch some, using different kinds of lines.

2. Draw some trees, making each tree's branches and leaves overlap to create a feeling of depth.

3. Fill your page, and touch all edges of the paper with your lines and shapes.

 Art Criticism

Describe What kind of trees did you draw?

Analyze How did overlapping help create a feeling of depth?

Interpret How would your drawing change if the trees did not overlap?

Decide How is your drawing like the paintings shown in the lesson? How is it different?

Lesson 4 Form

Look at the sculptures on these pages. *The Walking Flower* is a clay sculpture. The *Sun God* is a sculpture made from polyester. Form is an important element in both sculptures.

◀ **Fernand Leger.** (French). *The Walking Flower.* 1951.

Ceramic. $26\frac{1}{2} \times 20\frac{1}{2} \times 15$ inches ($67 \times 50 \times$ 38 cm.). Albright-Knox Art Gallery, Buffalo, New York.

 Art History and Culture

Artists use three-dimensional forms to create sculptures.

Study both sculptures to find the following forms.

▶ Find a form that has a circle or a shape of a circle painted on it.

▶ Locate forms that look like triangles.

▶ Find free-form shapes in these sculptures.

Aesthetic Perception

Design Awareness Look around your classroom. Find objects that have forms like the ones you found in the artwork.

Using Form

Shapes and forms are similar. They both can be geometric or free-form. But they are different, too. **Shapes** are flat and are **two-dimensional.** They can be measured in only two ways: height and width.

Forms are not flat. They are **three-dimensional** and can be measured in three ways: height, width, and depth.

Below are five basic forms. You saw them in the sculptures in this lesson. Which shapes do these forms remind you of?

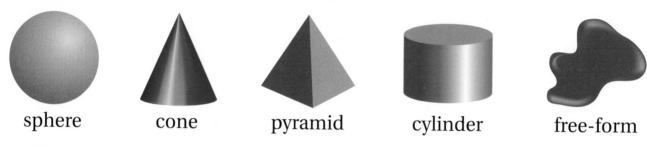

sphere   cone   pyramid   cylinder   free-form

Sculpture is three-dimensional art. The form of the sculpture is the positive space. The negative space is the area all around the sculpture.

Practice

Use a sheet of paper to make a form. It will have three dimensions.

1. Tear a sheet of paper in several places without tearing it completely apart.

2. Fold, bend, curl, and twist the paper to make a form. Notice that it has three dimensions: height, width and depth.

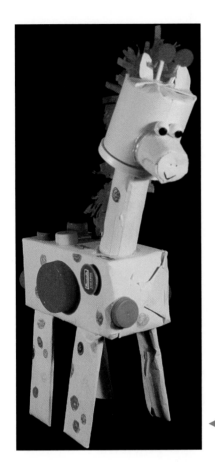

Think about how the sculpture appears to be three-dimensional.

◄ **Avery Terry.**
Age 8.

 **Creative Expression**

What objects around you have three dimensions? Create a three-dimensional paper sculpture.

1. Have you ever seen a sculpture shaped like an animal form?

2. Notice the sculptures *The Walking Flower* and *Sun God*. What are the similarities and differences?

3. Find objects outdoors to be used to create an animal.

4. Use a rectangular box or juice can for the body. Use pieces of cardboard for the legs. You can draw texture on your animal sculpture.

 **Art Criticism**

Describe What are the different materials you used to make your sculpture?

Analyze Point to the three dimensions in your sculpture. Identify the positive and negative spaces.

Interpret What does your sculpture make you think of?

Decide Why did you choose the animal form you used for the sculpture?

Relief Sculpture

Look at the artwork on these two pages. Both seem to have freestanding figures. *Presentation of Captives to a Maya Ruler* is a limestone relief sculpture which was created around A.D. 783. *Roman Hunting Scene* is also a relief sculpture that was created around the second century.

◀ **Artist Unknown.** (Mayan). *Presentation of Captives to a Maya Ruler.* c. 785.

Limestone with traces of paint. 45 $\frac{3}{8}$ × 35 inches (114 × 89 cm.). Kimbell Art Museum, Fort Worth, Texas.

 Art History and Culture

Artists create relief sculptures by making raised forms on flat surfaces. Reliefs are often used for decoration.

Study both works of art to find the following areas of relief.

▶ Find the areas that appear to be raised. Trace them with your finger.

▶ Where are the flat areas?

▶ Which relief seems to be the highest?

▶ In which work do the figures seem most realistic?

▲ **Artist Unknown.** (Roman). *Hunting Scene on Handle from a large bowl.* Second century or later.

Silver. 5 × 14 $\frac{3}{8}$ × 35 inches (13 × 38 × 89 cm.). The Metropolitan Museum of Art, New York, New York.

Aesthetic Perception

Design Awareness Look closely at both sides of a coin. Which areas are raised? Why do you think the background is empty?

Creating Relief Sculpture

relief sculpture

free standing sculpture

Artwork in which forms stand out from a flat surface is called **relief sculpture.**

Most three-dimensional sculptures are **freestanding.** They have empty, negative space all around them. Relief sculptures, however, are not freestanding. The background in a relief sculpture is flat, and the positive areas are raised.

Coins are one example of relief that we see every day. What other examples can you think of?

Practice

Write your name in relief. Use glue and yarn.

1. Make a design with thick lines of yarn glued onto a piece of paper.
2. Allow the glue to dry for a few hours.

◄ **Kourtney Axelberg.**
Age 7.

Think about how this student's relief sculpture is different from one that is freestanding.

Creative Expression

What would you like to show in a self-portrait? Create a self-portrait in relief tile.

1. Describe what is happening in both of the relief works. Do some of the areas appear to stick out more than others?

2. If you could make a relief sculpture that told a story about you, what would you put on the relief?

3. Roll out a slab of clay and create a relief of objects or a picture of a person who is important to you.

4. With a pencil draw the design into the clay. Press lightly so as not to cut through the clay.

Art Criticism

Describe What shapes did you use? What elements in the tile make it a relief?

Analyze Which areas are in relief? What are a few facts about the artwork?

Interpret What words would you use to describe your self-portrait? How would the work change if there were no raised areas?

Decide What do you like best about your relief? Why?

Three-Dimensional Art to Wear

Look at the necklace from Morocco and the necklace from the Ivory Coast. They are both forms of three-dimensional art. These pieces of jewelry also have raised areas and were made from a variety of materials.

▲ **Artist unknown.**
(Morocco). *Necklace.*
Twentieth century.
....
Beads and silver alloy.
14 inches long (35.5 cm.).
Private collection.

 Art History and Culture

A jeweler creates decorative, three-dimensional forms to wear.

◀ **Artist Unknown.**
(Ivory Coast). *Cote d' Ivoire.*
Gold. c. 1900
• • • • • • • • • • • • • • • • • •
118 $\frac{1}{2}$ inches (300 cm.).
Museum of Fine Arts,
Houston, Texas.

Study both works of art.

▶ Find areas where the designs are raised.

▶ What do you think the necklaces will sound like when worn?

▶ Find the free-form shapes.

▶ Where are the round shapes?

🔍 Aesthetic Perception

Seeing Like an Artist Look around your classroom. Is anyone wearing jewelry? What color is it?

Designing and Making Jewelry

A piece of **jewelry** is three-dimensional artwork that is made for people to wear. A **jeweler** is an artist who designs and makes jewelry. The art of making jewelry has been around for about 4000 years. Rings and necklaces are forms of jewelry. Can you think of any other forms?

Varieties of materials are used to make jewelry. Gold, silver, and gemstones are used most often. Jewelry can also be made with wood, glass, leather, beads, and paper. Can you think of any other materials that are used to make jewelry?

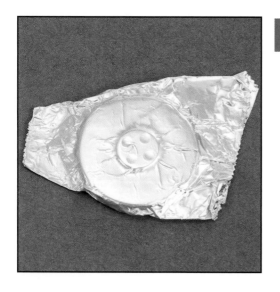

Practice

Use a found object and foil to practice making a foil relief.

1. Place foil on top of an object such as a button to get the feel of stretching foil gently. Start in the middle and use your fingers to gently press and smooth the foil across the flat surface and over the ridges.

2. Remove the foil from the object and you will have the object's impression.

◀ **Ashley Blake.**
Age 9.

Think about what makes a medallion a relief.

 **Creative Expression**

What type of jewelry would you like to wear? Create a medallion.

1. Think about small objects that have interesting shapes.

2. Cut a piece of cardboard into a geometric shape. Arrange objects on top of the cardboard in different ways. Glue your favorite arrangement to the cardboard.

3. When dry, cover the surface with foil.

4. Punch a hole at the top of your design. Pass a piece of yarn or ribbon through the hole, and tie the ends to make a necklace.

Art Criticism

Describe What objects did you use to create the raised areas of the relief?

Analyze What kind of shapes did you use to create your relief work?

Interpret When would you wear a medallion?

Decide If you could create another medallion, what would you change?

Space and Form

▲ **Rene Magritte.** (Belgian). *The Blank Signature (Carte Blance).* 1965.

Oil on canvas. 32 × 25 $\frac{1}{8}$ inches (81 × 64 cm.).
National Gallery of Art, Washington, D.C.

Art Criticism | Critical Thinking

Describe What do you see?

▶ What does the credit line tell you about the painting?

▶ Describe the woman and what she is doing.

▶ What is the setting?

Analyze How is this work organized?

▶ Where do you see positive shapes and negative spaces?

▶ What is in the foreground, middle ground, and background?

▶ Which objects seem to be closest, and which are farthest away?

▶ How did the artist use size and detail to show depth?

▶ What unusual trick has the artist played with space?

Interpret What is the artist trying to say?

▶ How does the artist's use of space and shape affect the look of this work?

▶ What do you think is happening in this painting? Write a brief paragraph explaining this image.

Decide What do you think about the work?

▶ Is this painting successful because it is realistic, because it is well-organized, or because it has a strong message? Explain.

Show What You Know

Answer these questions on a separate sheet of paper.

1 The area that shapes and forms fill is _____.
A. negative space
B. positive space
C. relief sculpture

2 Three-dimensional shapes are called _____.
A. jewelry
B. positive space
C. forms

3 The part of an artwork that appears farthest away is the _____.
A. background
B. foreground
C. relief

4 _____ is when one object covers part of another object.
A. Relief
B. Freestanding
C. Overlapping

5 The area between and around an object is _____.
A. negative space
B. relief
C. form

CAREERS IN ART
Architecture

Look around your neighborhood. What do the buildings look like? Are there parks? These things were designed to look the way they do.

Architects design buildings from houses to sports stadiums. Architects must think about how a building will be used as well as how it should look.

Landscape architects design green spaces. They must think about how the shapes and colors of different plants will look together.

City planners think about what kinds of housing, parking, and parks people will need.

▲ **Architect**

Space and Form in Animation

John Ramirez is an animator and storyboard artist. His video "Every Picture Tells a Story" shows how he works with a team to make animated films. He studies space and form in photographs to know how to draw scenes in his storyboards.

What to Do Tell a short story in a four-frame comic strip.

Comic strips are a simple form of storyboarding. They have four frames in which to tell a simple story. The style of art and the layout of the frames are important. They help show the story from beginning to end.

1. Think of a simple story. Your story should have characters and a beginning, a middle, and an end.

2. Sketch out four scenes that will show action in the story.

3. Use overlapping to create depth in your scenes. Name your characters. Add dialogue and a title.

4. Share your comic strip with friends. Ask them if they understand the story.

▲ John Ramirez and Paul Tracey. "Every Picture Tells a Story."

Art Criticism

Describe Describe the scenes you chose to show your story.

Analyze How did you choose the four scenes that would best tell your story?

Interpret How did you create depth in your drawings?

Decide Was there something you wanted in your story but couldn't quite achieve?

Color and Value

◀ **Diego Rivera.** (Mexican). *Kneeling Child on Yellow Background.* 1927.

• •

Oil on canvas. 25 $\frac{1}{2}$ × 21 inches (65 × 53 cm.). San Francisco Museum of Modern Art, San Francisco, California.

Artists use color and value to make their artwork special.

Diego Rivera was inspired by ancient Mexican sculpture forms. This painting shows a portrait of a young Mexican girl. It was made by mixing together different colors.

Artists use **color** to create a certain feeling or emotion in art.

▶ What colors do you see in *Kneeling Child on Yellow Background*?

▶ What do the colors make you think of?

Some artists use different **values** of a color to show the highlights and shadows of an object.

▶ Where did Rivera use light and dark color values on the young girl's face?

▶ Where else do you see light and dark values of a color?

Self-Portrait

Diego Rivera
(1886–1957)

Diego Rivera was born in Mexico. As a young boy, he loved to draw and paint. When he grew up, Rivera became famous for creating large murals on the sides of buildings and on walls. His murals show people in their struggle for a better life. These murals can be seen today in Mexico and the United States.

In This Unit you will learn about colors and the moods they create. You will practice mixing and using colors.

Here are the topics you will study:
▶ Primary and Secondary Colors
▶ Value
▶ Intermediate Colors
▶ Color Wheel
▶ Warm and Cool Colors
▶ Color Contrast

Looking at Color

Look at Shirley Russell's *Boy's Day*. It is about a holiday celebrated by flying flags and colorful streamers. *Piero's Piazza* painted by Al Held is an abstract painting. It is a tribute to a late fifteenth-century artist by the name of Piero della Francesca. Both artists use color to show the mood of the events they painted.

◀ **Shirley Ximena Hopper Russell.** (American). *Boys' Day.* 1935.

Oil on canvas. 29 $\frac{5}{8}$ × 24 $\frac{5}{8}$ inches (76 × 63.5 cm.). Honolulu Academy of Art, Honolulu, Hawaii.

 ## Art History and Culture

Look at the different colors in these two artworks. How did the artists use color to express different feelings or moods in the works of art?

Study both paintings to find the following colors.

▶ Find the primary colors—red, yellow, and blue.

▶ Point to the secondary colors—orange, green, and violet.

▶ Where are the light colors? The dark colors?

▲ **Al Held.** (American).
Piero's Piazza. 1982.

Acrylic on canvas. 96 $\frac{1}{2}$ ×
143 $\frac{7}{8}$ inches (244 × 366 cm.).
Albright-Knox Art Gallery,
Buffalo, New York.

Aesthetic Perception

Seeing Like an Artist Look in a magazine. Find the same colors that you saw in the paintings.

Using Colors

Colors are used to express different moods or feelings in works of art. **Hue** is another word for *color.* The three **primary colors** are red, yellow, and blue. They cannot be made by mixing colors.

The **secondary colors** are made by mixing two primary colors.

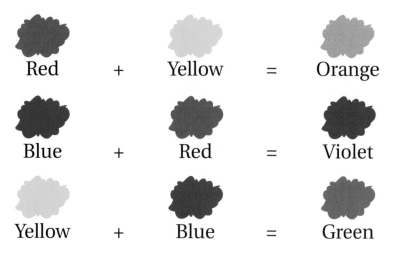

Red	+	Yellow	=	Orange
Blue	+	Red	=	Violet
Yellow	+	Blue	=	Green

Value is the lightness or darkness of a color. Adding white makes a color lighter. Adding black makes a color darker. When the value of a color is lighter, it is called a **tint.** When the value of a color is darker, it is called a **shade.**

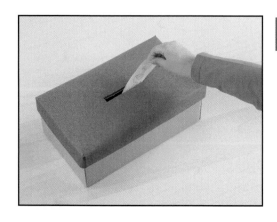

Practice

Hold a "Color Bee."

1. Divide into four teams. Think up color questions based on the above information.

2. Write each question on a piece of paper. Fold the papers and put them into a question box.

3. Take turns pulling questions from the box and answering them.

◀ **Domenique Chery.** Age 8.

Think about how this student artist created mood in her artwork.

 **Creative Expression**

What colors do you like? Draw a picture of a special event using colors that show the feeling of that event.

1. Think of ways that you, your family, and friends celebrate special events. Choose one event for your drawing. What colors will you need to include? What colors will you use to show the mood of this event?

2. Draw the event or occasion with colored markers on white construction paper.

3. Fill your paper with color.

Art Criticism

Describe What special event did you draw? Describe the people and objects. Point to the tints and shades.

Analyze Name the colors you used. Did you use some colors for special effects?

Interpret What is the mood of your event?

Decide If you could make this drawing again, how would you improve it?

Intermediate Colors

▲ **Artist Unknown.** (Peru).
Hat: Birds and Geometric Patterns. 700–1000 A.D.

Alpaca and cotton. $4\frac{1}{2} \times 5$ inches
(11 × 13 cm.). The Seattle Art
Museum, Seattle, Washington.

Look at the two works of art on these pages. Both artists used intermediate colors in their works of art.

 Art History and Culture

Hat is woven from Alpaca wool. This wool makes a very fine woven cloth. Alpacas are raised in many countries, including the United States and Australia.

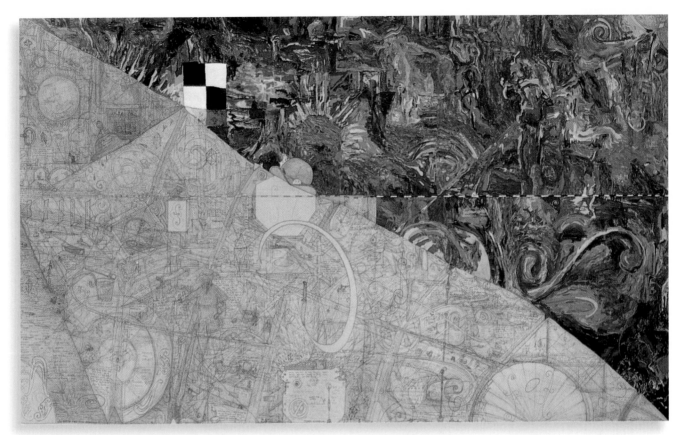

Study both works of art to find the intermediate colors.

▶ Find the yellow-orange hues. Where are the red-orange hues?

▶ What other intermediate colors can you find?

▲ **William T. Wiley.**
(American). *Remedial Archaeology and the Like.* 1986.

100 × 165 inches (254 × 419 cm.).
Acrylic and graphite on canvas.
Birmingham Museum of Art,
Birmingham, Alabama.

Aesthetic Perception

Seeing Like an Artist Look through this unit. Find more examples of the colors you saw in the art on these pages.

Using Intermediate Colors

Intermediate colors are made by mixing a **primary color** and a **secondary color.** There are six intermediate colors—red-orange, yellow-orange, yellow-green, blue-green, blue-violet, and red-orange.

A **color wheel** is an artist's way of organizing these 12 colors.

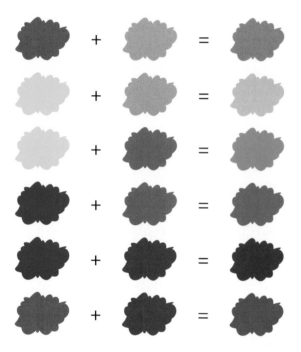

Practice

Browse magazines to find intermediate colors. Then use scissors to cut out each color.

1. Fold a sheet of paper into six equal boxes. Write the name of one intermediate color in each box.

2. Glue each example from the magazines into the correct box.

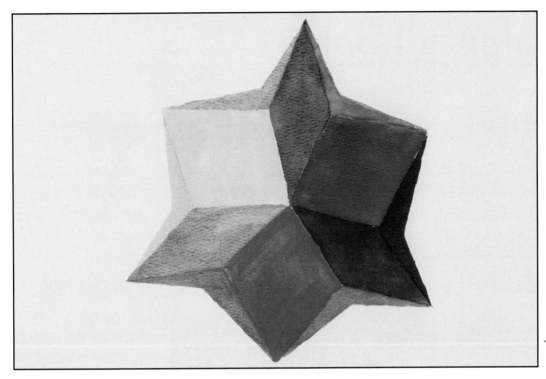

◀ **Alex Bryan.**
Age 9.

Think about what colors you like. Which colors do you like that are bright or dark? What colors do you like that can create a mood?

Creative Expression

Design your own unique color wheel using primary, secondary, and intermediate colors.

1. The colors must be in the correct order.

2. Use primary paint colors to mix secondary and intermediate colors.

3. The wheel does not have to be round, or even a circle.

4. Plan and decide a way to indicate the difference between primary, secondary, and intermediate colors.

Art Criticism

Describe What step did you follow to make your unique color wheel?

Analyze Name the primary, secondary, and intermediate colors in the color wheel.

Interpret Do any of the intermediate colors make you feel a certain way or put you in a particular mood?

Decide Which of the intermediate colors look the best? Which would you recreate? Why?

Look at the works of art on these pages. Both artists have used spectral colors. *La Fortune* was painted by Man Ray in 1938. About the same time, Calvin Jones created *Brilliant as the Sun Upon the World.*

▲ **Man Ray.** (American).
La Fortune. 1938.
....
Oil on canvas. 24 × 29 inches (61 × 74 cm.). Whitney Museum of Art, New York, New York.

 Art History and Culture

Jones's painting contains many symbols and patterns of Africa. How many can you identify?

Study the colors used in both works of art.

▶ Find the primary colors.

▶ Where are the secondary colors?

▶ Which artist used intermediate colors?

▲ **Calvin Jones.**
(American). *Brilliant as the Sun Upon the World.* c. 1950.
. . . .
Private Collection.

Aesthetic Perception

Seeing Like an Artist Look around to see how many colors of the spectrum you can find.

Using a Color Wheel

The range of colors that comes from light is called the **color spectrum.** Rainbows are the most famous display of this spectrum in nature. The spectrum that artists use is bent into the shape of a circle. It is called a color wheel.

The color wheel includes the six spectral colors and six intermediate colors. Like the colors in the spectrum, these colors are always placed in the same order, no matter which way you turn the wheel.

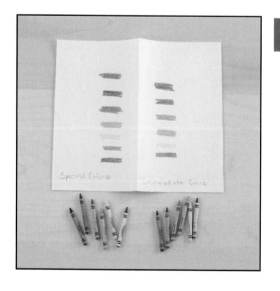

Practice

Use crayons to create a color chart.

1. Divide a sheet of paper in half. Label one side "Spectral Colors" and the other side "Intermediate Colors".

2. Use crayons to show the colors in spectral order on each side.

◀ **Savannah Valentine.** Age 8.

Think about this student's amusement ride. What colors did she use?

 **Creative Expression**

What is your favorite amusement ride? Create an amusement ride for the Rainbow Park using the color wheel.

1. Think about an amusement ride you can make using all the colors from a color wheel in order.

2. Be creative. Remember that the colors have to follow the order of the color wheel.

 **Art Criticism**

Describe What kind of ride did you create?

Analyze How did you organize your colors?

Interpret Give your ride a name.

Decide Did you make an interesting ride?

Cool Colors

Look at both works of art. They were created by twentieth-century artists. Milton Avery believed aesthetic composition should dominate his work. Wayne Thiebaud was concerned with realism. Both artists emphasized the use of cool colors in these paintings.

◄ **Wayne Thiebaud.** (American).
Lighted City. 1987.
....
Gouache and charcoal on paper. 29 × 20 inches
(74 × 51 cm.). Private Collection.

 Art History and Culture

Look at these two works of art that show different outdoor scenes. How did the two artists use cool colors to suggest a calm emotion or feeling?

▲ **Milton Avery.** (American).
Sea Grasses and Blue Sea.
1958.

Oil on canvas. 60 $\frac{1}{8}$ × 6 $\frac{3}{8}$ inches (152.4 × 15.24 cm.). The Museum of Modern Art, New York, New York.

Study both works of art to find the following cool colors.

▶ Find the different kinds of blue.

▶ Find the intermediate colors blue-green and blue-violet.

▶ How do the cool colors affect the mood of each painting?

Aesthetic Perception

Seeing Like an Artist Look through magazines to find pictures of blue, green, and violet objects in nature. Write down what you see.

Using Cool Colors

Blue, green, and violet are considered **cool colors.** They can remind us of cool objects such as grass, water, and ice. Yellow-green, green, blue-green, blue, violet, and blue-violet are colors that are related, like members of a family. You can find them on a color wheel to see what they have in common.

Practice

Create a drawing using cool colors. Use crayons and white paper.

1. Write these words on a sheet of paper: *ocean, sky, grapes, grass, leaves,* and *lettuce.*

2. On the same sheet of paper, create a drawing that includes each of the objects listed above. Use the correct cool colors to color the objects.

◀ **Jenna Mooney.**
Age 8.

Think about a name for this student artist's sculpture that ties its cool colors with the environment.

Creative Expression

Where in your environment do you see cool colors? Design a sculpture of an environment using cool colors.

1. Think of ideas dealing with your environment, such as an animal habitat or a playground in the year 3001. Choose an idea and then sketch a few things you would find there.

2. Select several pieces of cool-colored paper. Choose one piece for the base. Outline objects you want in your environment on the other sheets of paper and cut them out. Add detail with oil pastels in cool colors. Attach the objects to your base.

Art Criticism

Describe Describe your environment. What objects did you use? How did you decide where to place them?

Analyze Which cool colors did you use?

Interpret How did using only cool colors affect the mood of your environment?

Decide If you could redo your sculpture, what would you do? What colors would you add?

Warm Colors

▲ **Paul Klee.** (Swiss).
Rotes Haus. 1929.

Oil on canvas mounted on cardboard.
$10 \times 10\frac{7}{8}$ inches (25 × 28 cm.). San
Francisco Museum of Modern Art, San
Francisco, California.

Look at the works of art on these two pages. *Rotes Haus* means "red house." Georgia O'Keeffe created *Red Canna,* which means "red flower," around 1925. Both artists used warm colors in their artwork.

 Art History and Culture

Which work of art is strictly imaginary, and which one is based on observation?

Study both works of art to find the following warm colors.

▶ Find the spectral hues red, orange, and yellow.

▶ Where are the intermediate hues red-orange and yellow-orange?

▶ How would you describe the mood or feeling of each piece?

Aesthetic Perception

Seeing Like an Artist Look at what your classmates are wearing. Find examples of warm hues like those you saw in the artwork.

Using Warm Colors

Warm colors are the **spectral colors** yellow, orange, and red that give a sense of warmth in a work of art. They can be found opposite the cool colors on the color wheel.

Red-violet, red, red-orange, orange, yellow-orange, and yellow are warm colors that are related. They remind many people of warm or hot things like fire and the sun.

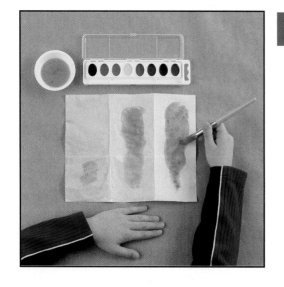

Practice

Mix a variety of warm colors. Use watercolor paints, brushes, and white paper.

1. Fold your sheet of paper into three equal parts. Paint the first box red, the middle box orange, and the last box yellow.

2. While the paint is still wet, add different amounts of violet to the red box, then mix.

3. In the same way, add and mix red in the orange box, and orange in the yellow box.

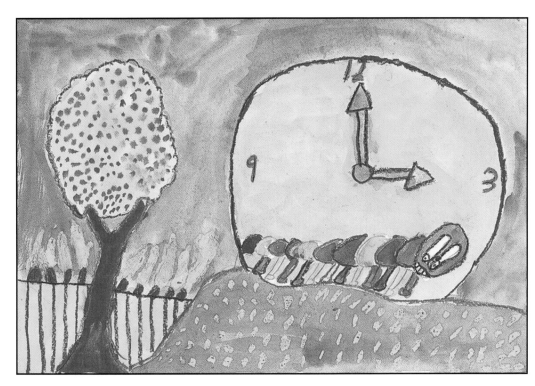

Think about what makes this student artwork imaginary.

Creative Expression

What colors in your environment give you a feeling of warmth? Create an imaginative painting using warm colors.

1. Use your imagination to create a fantasy landscape that includes three unrelated items such as a matchstick, a bowling pin, and a pair of sunglasses. Make a rough sketch of your idea.

2. Use lines to draw your idea on a sheet of white paper with warm-colored oil pastels.

3. Mix a variety of warm values with watercolor paint. Paint your scene. Remember that the values will get lighter as you add more water to your paint.

Art Criticism

Describe What objects did you include in your imaginative painting?

Analyze Name the warm colors you used in your landscape.

Interpret How did using only warm colors affect the mood of your imaginative painting? How would adding cool colors change the mood?

Decide If you could do this artwork over again, how would you improve it?

Color Contrast

◀ **Idelle Weber.** (American).
Pistia Kew. 1989.

Oil on linen. 58 × 59 inches (147
× 150 cm.). Schmidt Bingham
Gallery, New York, New York.

Look at the artwork on these pages. *Pistia Kew* was
painted by Idelle Weber in 1989. *Covered Jar* was
created in China about 400 years ago. Both works
show a contrast of warm and cool colors.

 Art History and Culture

Idelle Weber is best known for painting realistic objects seen
in everyday environments.

◀ **Artist Unknown.**
(China). *Covered Jar.*
1522–1566.
....
Porcelain painted with underglaze
cobalt blue and overglaze enamels.
18 $\frac{1}{2}$ inches high, 15 $\frac{3}{4}$ inches in
diameter (46.99 cm. high, 40 cm. in
diameter). Asia Society of New York,
New York.

Study both works of art to find the contrast between warm and cool colors.

▶ Find all the cool colors. Are they placed near each other?

▶ Locate all the warm colors.

Aesthetic Perception

Seeing Like an Artist Look around your classroom and find examples of cool colors that are near warm colors.

Using Color Contrast

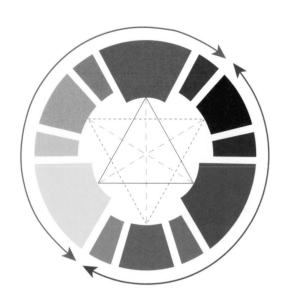

Artists use **contrast** in order to show differences between two things.

The **warm colors** red, orange, and yellow come forward and attract your attention first. So do their related intermediate colors. The **cool colors** blue, green, and violet—and their related intermediate colors—seem to move away from you.

When warm colors are placed next to cool colors, a contrast is created.

Practice

Illustrate color contrast. Use oil pastels and white paper.

1. On a sheet of paper, place cool colors next to warm colors.

2. Mix the intermediate colors by blending the primary and secondary colors. Fill your paper with color contrasts.

Art Criticism Critical Thinking

Describe **What do you see?**

During this step you will collect information about the subject of the work.

▶ What does the credit line tell you about the painting?

▶ What objects do you see?

Analyze **How is this work organized?**

Think about how the artist has used the elements and principles of art.

▶ Where do you see primary colors?

▶ What secondary colors do you see? Point them out.

Interpret **What is the artist trying to say?**

Use the clues you discovered during your analysis to find the message the artist is trying to show.

▶ What is out of the ordinary in this painting?

▶ Imagine that you are the manager of a store that sells these goodies. Write an advertisement for the local paper that will make people want to come.

Decide **What do you think about the work?**

Use all the information you have gathered to decide whether this is a successful work of art.

▶ Is this painting successful because it is realistic, because it is well organized, or because if has a strong message. Explain your answer.

Color and Value, continued

Show What You Know

Answer these questions on a separate sheet of paper.

1 These colors are considered pure colors. _____
  A. secondary colors
  B. tricolor
  C. primary colors

2 The lightness or darkness of a color is called _____.
  A. color
  B. value
  C. shade

3 This tool is used to organize the twelve colors. _____
  A. organizing tool
  B. circle of colors
  C. color wheel

4 Yellow-green and blue-green are colors that remind us of cool things. These color are called _____.
  A. warm colors
  B. chill colors
  C. cool colors

5 Which word is used to show differences between two things?
_____
  A. comparing
  B. contrast
  C. difference

VISIT A MUSEUM
The Museum of Fine Arts

The Museum of Fine Arts in Houston, Texas, is the largest art museum in the Southwest. Its collection contains over 27,000 works of art. There you can see examples of styles of art from different periods in history. There is also a large collection of American decorative arts including furniture, paintings, metals, ceramics, glass, and textiles. If you visit the museum, you can walk in the sculpture garden and see sculptures created by many nineteenth- and twentieth-century artists.

Color and Value

"The Story of Babar, the Little Elephant"

Color and value are important elements for artists. Both costume and set designers also choose a color palette when they work on a play. In the theatre production of *The Story of Babar, the Little Elephant*, the director wanted the colors to match the book illustrations that inspired the play.

What to Do Create tableaux using illustrations from a book.

Adapting a book into a play requires a lot of work. This work is done by a team of creative people, including a playwright, director, costume designer, set designer, and actors. You will work as set and costume designers for a scene in a play.

1. Choose a children's picture book.

2. Select an illustration that shows a specific setting and characters.

3. Select an emotion that captures the story's theme. Then select a palette of colors that expresses that emotion.

4. Your group will design both the set and the costumes for your scene. Divide the jobs of designing costumes and sets, but work with the same palette of colors.

5. Present your ideas to the class.

▲ Children's Theatre Company. "The Story of Babar, the Little Elephant."

 Art Criticism

Describe What challenges did you face in getting your group to make decisions?

Analyze What was interesting about using a specific palette of colors for both costumes and sets?

Interpret How did your palette of colors express the emotion you chose?

Decide In designing the costumes and set, did you stay true to the colors and values you chose as your palette?

Texture and Balance

Artists use **texture** and **balance** to design works of art and to show how objects may feel.

▲ **Audrey Flack.** (American). *Strawberry Tart Supreme.* 1974.

Oil over acrylic on canvas. $54 \times 60 \frac{1}{4}$ inches (137.16 × 153.04 cm). Allen Memorial Art Museum, Oberlin, Ohio.

Artists can create **texture** in a work of art to show how things might feel if they were touched.

▶ What textures do you see in *Strawberry Tart Supreme*?

▶ Artists use balance in their artwork to give equal weight to both sides of a design.

▶ Are both sides of the painting exactly the same? If not, what are some differences?

In This Unit you will learn about texture and balance, and how other artists use these features in their designs. Here are the topics you will study:

▶ Formal Balance
▶ Formal Balance in Masks
▶ Symmetry
▶ Approximate Symmetry
▶ Visual Texture
▶ Tactile Texture

Audrey Flack

(1931–)

Audrey Flack always knew she wanted to be an artist. She is a native of New York City, where she attended Music and Art High School. She studied with Josef Albers at Yale and started her career as an abstract expressionist. Her desire to do realistic work brought her back to New York, where she studied at The Art Student's League and NYU.

In the mid-1960s she made paintings of famous people. During the 1970s she used photography to help her create monumental still lifes like *Strawberry Tart Supreme.* During the 1980s she created sculptures about heroic women and goddess figures.

Formal Balance

◀ **Horace Pippin.**
(American).
Victorian Parlor II.
1945.
....
Oil on canvas. 25 $\frac{1}{4}$ × 30
inches (63.5 × 76.2 cm.).
The Metropolitan
Museum of Art,
New York.

Look at the works of art on these pages. Folk artists
are self taught. *Jar* was created 700 years before
Victorian Parlor II, yet both works make powerful
use of formal balance.

 Art History and Culture

Many of Horace Pippin's works of art depict his childhood
memories of war experiences, heroes, and religious
experiences.

Study each artwork to see balance.

▶ Draw a line down the middle of each artwork with your finger. Describe the matching objects or shapes you see on the two sides.

▶ Describe colors that are repeated in both works of art.

▶ Which areas are exactly the same on both sides of each piece?

▶ Which areas are similar but not exactly the same?

◀ **Artist Unknown.** (China). *Jar.* Northern Song Period, twelfth century.
....
Stoneware with graffito design in slip under glaze. 12 $\frac{1}{2}$ inches (31.75 cm.). The Asian Society, New York, New York.

Aesthetic Perception

Seeing Like an Artist Look for a building in the area where you live that has the same colors and forms on its left and right halves. What features are alike, but not exactly the same?

Using Formal Balance

Formal balance is a way of organizing a design so that equal or similar elements are placed on opposite sides of an imaginary central dividing line. You saw examples of formal balance in the artwork on pages 126 and 127.

On a seesaw, if your partner is much bigger than you, you will stay up in the air. The seesaw is not balanced. But if your partner is your weight, the seesaw will balance. There is the same amount of weight on both sides.

A work of art can have different kinds of balance. One kind is formal balance. This is created when objects, shapes, lines, and color match on both sides of a design.

Practice

Illustrate formal balance. Use a pencil.

1. Fold a piece of paper in half and then open it again. Use a pencil to draw some geometric and free-form shapes on the left side.

2. Repeat the same design on the right side to create formal balance.

◀ **Keegan Faught.**
Age 9.

Think about where this student used formal balance.

Creative Expression

How do buildings show formal balance? Use formal balance in drawing.

1. Look at the artwork *Victorian Parlor II* by Horace Pippin. Think about how the outside of this house might look.

2. On a large piece of paper, draw the outside of the house. Use formal balance in your drawing.

3. Fill the house with color. Add trees and plants. Use formal balance in your landscape too.

Art Criticism

Describe What objects did you include in your drawing?

Analyze How did you create formal balance in your drawing?

Interpret How would the mood or feeling of your drawing change if you had not used formal balance?

Decide If you could redo this drawing, what would you do differently?

Formal Balance in Masks

Look at the three-dimensional masks. *Senufo Face Mask* was created between the nineteenth and twentieth centuries. *Mask with Seal or Sea Otter Spirit* was created around the nineteenth century. Both artists used formal balance to design their masks.

◀ **Artist Unknown.** (Ivory Coast). *Senufo Face Mask.* Nineteenth to twentieth century.
....
Wood, horn, fiber, cloth, feather, metal. 14 $\frac{1}{2}$ inches tall (35.56 cm.). The Metropolitan Museum of Art, New York, New York.

 Art History and Culture

Many Eskimos hunt for food because they have developed a widespread knowledge of animals such as the sea otter, seal, and bear.

Study both masks to find examples of formal balance.

▶ What shapes do you see on each mask?

▶ Find shapes or objects on the left side that you also see on the right.

▶ Find areas on both sides that are exactly the same.

▶ Are any areas on either side similar, but not quite the same?

Aesthetic Perception

Seeing Like an Artist Look at posters and signs in your school to find examples of formal balance.

Using Formal Balance in Masks

People in many **cultures** around the world make and use masks. Ancient hunters wore animal masks in hunting ceremonies. Storytellers and actors wear masks to portray different characters.

The features on masks are often **exaggerated,** or made larger, to show strong feelings.

The masks below have formal balance. They have the same shapes and objects on both sides of an imaginary dividing line.

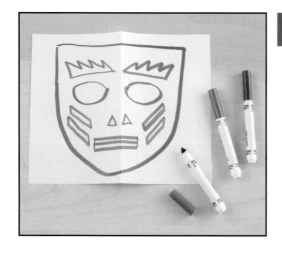

Practice

Design a paper mask with exaggerated features that are formally balanced. Use colored markers.

1. Fold a piece of paper in half, and then open it to mark the middle of the mask.

2. Think of an emotion you want the mask to express. Sketch exaggerated features that express that emotion. Use free-form and geometric shapes. The features on each side of the fold should look alike in some way.

◀ **Alexander Jimenez.**
Age 9.

Think about how this student artist's mask shows formal balance.

 **Creative Expression**

Which features in a mask would show formal balance? Create a papier-mâché mask. Use formal balance.

1. Think of how you want to use your mask and what it will express. Make a few sketches until you get one you like.

2. Look at your sketch. Then cut pieces of cardboard tubes and boxes to form the features. Tape or glue them in place onto your base. Balance some of the forms formally.

3. Dip torn strips of newspaper into paste. Apply them to the mask.

Art Criticism

Describe List the steps you followed to create your mask.

Analyze Which parts of your mask show formal balance?

Interpret What feeling does the finished mask express?

Decide Which elements of the mask do you like best? How is the finished mask different from your sketch?

Symmetry

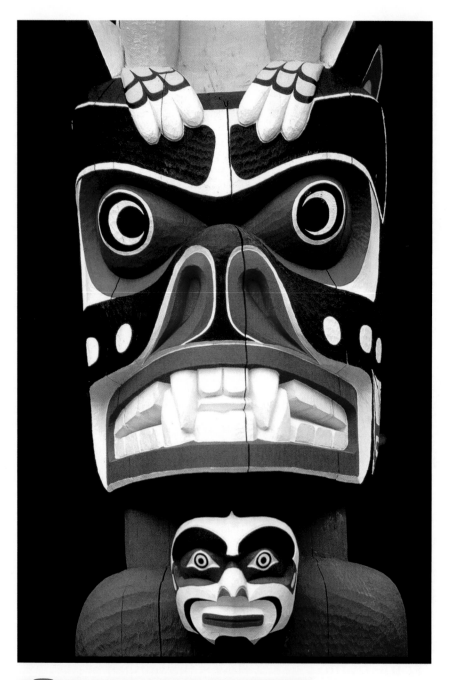

Look at *Totem Pole* and *Candelabra*. Both use formal balance. This totem comes from Native Americans of the Northwest Coast. A totem is a sacred symbol of one or more animals whose spirits protect a family clan. *Candelabra* was created in Mexico. It was used by a family during a religious ceremony announcing the engagement of a young couple.

◀ **Artist Unknown.** *Symmetrical View of a Totem Pole.*

Stanley Park, Vancouver, British Columbia, Canada.

 Art History and Culture

A totem pole was often placed in front of a home as a symbol of protection.

Study both works of art to find examples of symmetry.

► What single shape or object do you see in the center of each work?

► Find the shapes that are exactly the same on both sides of the center line.

► What colors are repeated in exactly the same place on both sides of each sculpture?

◄ **Aurelio and Francisco Flores.**
(Mexico). *Candelabra.* c. 1980.
....
Hand molded, fired, painted; clay, paint, wire.
42 × 26 × 8 $\frac{1}{4}$ inches (106.68 × 66.04 × 20.96
cm.). Museum of International Folk Art, Santa Fe,
New Mexico.

Aesthetic Perception

Seeing Like an Artist Look at the works of art in this book to find other examples of symmetry.

Using Symmetry

These artists used symmetry to create designs on the totem pole and candleholder. **Symmetry** is a special type of formal balance in which two halves of a design are identical, or mirror images of each other. The two halves are divided by a **central axis,** which is an imaginary dividing line. Everything on one side of the central axis is balanced by the objects on the other side. Artists use symmetry when they want designs to look formal and important.

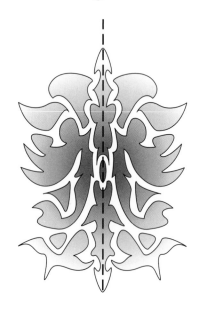

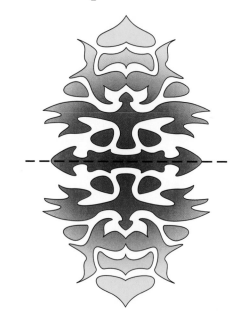

Practice

Use a balance scale to create perfect balance. Use a variety of materials.

1. Practice using formal balance by adding and taking away a variety of materials on each side of the scale.

◀ **Donald Nguyen.**
Age 9.

Think about the central axis in this totem and how it runs down the center of the face.

Creative Expression

What images would you put on a totem pole? Use symmetry to create a totem.

1. Think of a real or imaginary creature. Make several sketches.

2. Fold a sheet of paper in half. The fold will be your central axis.

3. Using small pieces of colored paper, cut out shapes to represent features such as eyes. Using symmetry, place these features on your totem. Glue the pieces into place.

4. Use symmetry to add other details.

5. Join the edges of your paper together to form a cylinder.

Art Criticism

Describe What creature did you choose for your totem? What kinds of shapes did you use?

Analyze How did you create symmetrical balance?

Interpret What kind of feeling does the formal balance give your totem?

Decide If you could create another totem, what would you do differently?

Approximate Symmetry

Look at the portraits on these pages. *Portrait of a Boy* is a painting from an Egyptian mummy case. It was created more than 1,800 years ago. *Her World* was painted in 1948. Both artists used approximate symmetry to create these portraits. When something is symmetrical, it is the same on both sides. *Approximate symmetry* means that something is almost the same on both sides.

◀ **Artist Unknown.** (Egypt). *Portrait of a Boy.* Second century.

Encaustic on wood. 15 × 7 $\frac{1}{2}$ inches (38 × 19 cm.). The Metropolitan Museum of Art, New York, New York.

 Art History and Culture

Encaustic paint is made by mixing color pigment with wax.

Study each painting to find the following examples of approximate symmetry.

▶ Which features on the left side of the face are exactly the same as the ones on the right?

▶ Locate the shapes that are almost the same on both sides of the face.

▶ In which portrait is the hair the same on both sides?

◀ **Philip Evergood.** (American). *Her World.* 1948.

Oil on canvas. 48 × 35 $\frac{5}{8}$ (18.90 × 14.17 cm.). The Metropolitan Museum of Art, New York, New York.

 Aesthetic Perception

Seeing Like an Artist Look at a friend's face to find examples of approximate symmetry.

Using Approximate Symmetry

Approximate symmetry is a special kind of formal balance that happens when both sides of a design are *almost* exactly the same. The human face has approximate symmetry. Each side is almost the same as the other.

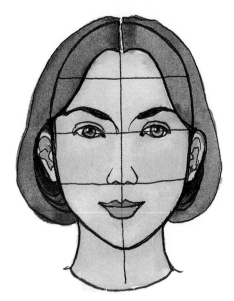

When drawing a portrait, it is helpful to draw the shape of the head first. Look at the guide lines in the face above. Notice that the eyes are placed about halfway between the top of the head and the bottom of the chin. Where are the tops of the ears? The nose? The mouth? What about your own face?

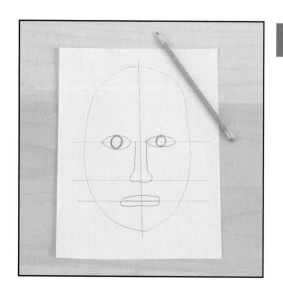

Practice

Illustrate approximate symmetry. Use a pencil.

1. Create the shape of a head by drawing a large oval shape. Draw a line *down* the middle of the shape and also *across* the middle.

2. Look at the guide lines in the diagram above to help you place the eyes, nose, mouth, and ears.

Think about how this student artist created approximate symmetry.

◀ **Maribel Cardinas.**
Age 9.

Creative Expression

What parts of your face show approximate symmetry? Use approximate symmetry in a self-portrait.

1. Look at your face in the mirror. Notice how it is almost exactly the same on both sides.

2. Use approximate symmetry to draw a self-portrait.

3. Add color.

Art Criticism

Describe What shapes did you use to create the face? What objects are included in the background?

Analyze How did you create approximate symmetry?

Interpret Give your portrait a title that expresses the emotions in the face.

Decide If you had painted this self-portrait a year ago, what objects would you have included?

Visual Texture

Look at the paintings on these two pages. *Paris Street Rainy Day* and *Diner* are paintings of city scenes. Both depict textures so accurately you can tell what all the surfaces would feel like if you could touch them.

▲ **Gustave Caillebotte.**
(French). *Paris Street Rainy Day.* 1877.
....
Oil on canvas. 83 $\frac{1}{2}$ × 108 $\frac{3}{4}$ inches
(210.82 × 274.32 cm.). Art Institute of Chicago, Chicago, Illinois.

 Art History and Culture

Caillebotte combined the realistic style of the academics with the everyday themes and viewpoints of the Impressionists.

▲ **Richard Estes.**
(American). *Diner.* 1971.
. . . .
Oil on canvas. 40 × 50 inches
(102.87 × 127 cm.).
Hirshhorn Museum and Sculpture
Garden, Smithsonian Institution,
Washington, D.C.

Study both paintings to find visual textures.

▶ Find the textures that look smooth.

▶ Where are the shiny-looking textures?

▶ Find the bumpy textures.

▶ Do you see textures that are smooth and dull?

Aesthetic Perception

Seeing Like an Artist Find the shiniest object in your classroom. What makes it look shiny?

Using Visual Texture

Visual texture is texture that you see with your eyes.

Lightly rub the surface of the pictures with your fingers. You cannot actually *feel* the different textures. You feel the smoothness of the paper instead.

If you have felt these textures before, you probably remember how they feel. Your eyes "see" the textures even though you cannot feel them. This is called visual texture.

Artists show shiny surfaces by using highlights. **Highlights** are small areas of white used to show the brightest spots on an object.

Practice

Make a rubbing of a texture to illustrate visual texture. Use a pencil.

1. Find an example of texture in your classroom.

2. Place a sheet of paper on top of the object.

3. Use the side of a pencil tip to rub the paper to create a visual texture.

◀ **Peter Olguin.**
Age 10.

Think about how this artist showed trees, bushes, and a sidewalk in his artwork.

 **Creative Expression**

Think about the area outside your house and the area around it.

1. Make a few quick sketches to show what your house looks like. Include things around your house like sidewalks, bushes, trees, or fences.

2. Now use the draw tool in the paint program to draw a picture of your house and the area around it. Think about the textures that are visible, such as rough bricks, glassy windows, or prickly bushes.

3. Use the fill tool and the texture tool to add color and texture to the drawing.

Art Criticism

Describe List the steps you followed to create this picture.

Analyze Describe the texture you created with the computer.

Interpret Give your work an expressive title.

Decide Were you successful in creating a variety of textures using the computer?

Tactile Texture

◄ **Ayako Miyawaki.** (Japanese). *Various Fish.* 1967.

13 × 11 ¾ inches (33.02 × 29.85 cm.). Cotton collage on burlap. The National Museum of Women in the Arts, Washington, D.C.

Look at *Thunderbird Shield* and *Various Fish.* The shield was created to wear when hunting or fighting and in special ceremonies. Both artists used a number of tactile textures in their work.

 Art History and Culture

Why do you think the artist created *Various Fish*?

◄ **Artist Unknown.** (American).
Thunderbird Shield. c. 1830.
. . . .
Buffalo-hide shield with inner cover, decorated with
paintings and feathers. Smithsonian National Museum of
the American Indian, New York, New York.

Study both works of art to find the tactile textures.

▶ Locate the smooth fabrics and the smooth-
   looking animal skin.

▶ Find the bumpy lines and dots made with string.
   How would they feel if you could touch them?

▶ Which artwork was made to look at, and which
   was made for a particular function?

Aesthetic Perception

Seeing Like an Artist Look through the works of art in this
book. Find a piece that includes real textures.

Using Tactile Texture

Tactile texture is the way the surface of an object actually feels when you touch it. It is an important element in many forms of art. Tactile textures are often the first things noticed in sculptures, jewelry, and weavings. Textured papers and fabrics make surfaces more interesting. Materials such as feathers and sand in a painting call attention to the rich variety of textures in our world.

Some artists use appliqué to create tactile texture. **Appliqué** is an art form in which cutout fabrics are attached to a larger surface.

Architects use tactile textures such as wood, brick, glass, and stone in the design of buildings.

Interior designers use tactile textures in furniture, carpets, and curtains to decorate the inside of a building. What textures are on the outside of the building where you live? What textures do you have in your bedroom or kitchen?

Practice

Look carefully at tactile textures in your clothing.

1. Find different textures in your clothing.

2. Describe how each texture feels when you touch it.

Think about this appliqué. Does the appliqué banner tell you about the student artist?

◀ **Chelsea Price.** Age 8.

 Creative Expression

What symbol would you choose to represent yourself? Design and stitch an appliqué banner.

1. Think about symbols that represent you. Make several sketches.

2. Choose your best sketch as a model. Cut out shapes from colorful fabric. Arrange them on a piece of burlap.

3. Attach shapes using glue and add details with a marker.

 **Art Criticism**

Describe List the symbols you put on your banner.

Analyze Describe the tactile textures in your work.

Interpret How do the symbols in the banner represent you?

Decide What do you like best about your artwork?

Texture and Balance

▲ **Henri Rousseau.** (French).
The Football Players. 1908.

Oil on canvas. 39 $\frac{1}{2}$ × 31 $\frac{5}{8}$ inches (100.33 × 81.28 cm.).
Solomon R. Guggenheim Museum, New York, New York.

 **Art Criticism** | **Critical Thinking**

Describe **What do you see?**

▶ What does the caption tell you about this work?

▶ Describe what you see.

Analyze **How is this work organized?**

▶ Where do you see symmetry or formal balance?

▶ Where do you see approximate symmetry?

▶ Where do you see visual texture?

▶ How has the artist used visual texture to make the trees in the foreground different from the trees in the middle ground and background?

Interpret **What is the artist trying to say?**

▶ What is happening in this painting?

▶ How can you tell whether the players are enjoying themselves?

▶ Is this football as you know it? Explain.

▶ Why do you think the artist showed only four players?

Decide **What do you think about the work?**

▶ Is this painting successful because it is realistic, well organized, or because it has a strong message? Explain.

Texture and Balance, continued

Show What You Know

Answer these questions on a separate sheet of paper.

1. To organize a design so equal elements are placed on each side of a central dividing line, use _____.
   A. approximate symmetry
   B. formal balance
   C. contrast in shape

2. The kind of formal balance in which both sides of a design are exactly the same is _____.
   A. emphasis
   B. formal balance
   C. symmetry

3. A special kind of formal balance in which both sides of a design are almost exactly the same is _____.
   A. rhythm
   B. approximate symmetry
   C. texture

4. Texture that you see is _____.
   A. visual texture
   B. tactile texture
   C. texture

5. The way a surface actually feels when touched is called _____.
   A. tactile texture
   B. visual rhythm
   C. textronics

VISIT A MUSEUM
The Walker Art Center

The Walker Art Center, located in Minneapolis, Minnesota, is famous for its collection of 8,000 pieces of twentieth-century art. The collection includes paintings, sculpture, videos, prints, drawings, and photographs. The Walker Art Center also has a varied educational program that appeals to people of all ages. Beside the museum is the Minneapolis Sculpture Garden. It covers eleven acres and is one of the largest urban sculpture parks in the country. It is a popular tourist attraction.

Texture and Balance in Music

Voice of the Wood is a play adapted from a book. The story is about a craftsman who makes a cello from the wood of an ancient tree. He searches for the one musician who can play the cello with such beautiful feelings that he or she can unlock the "voice of the wood."

What to Do Write a story about an instrument.

Think about a musical instrument you find interesting. Write a story about it. The instrument in your story can be a character or a prop. The story could be about a musician, a child searching for an instrument to play, or an instrument with a problem. Think about the characters, what they want or need, and where the story takes place. Have a clear beginning, middle, and end.

1. Write a story about an instrument.

2. Decide if the instrument is one of the characters or is a prop in the story.

3. How does your instrument sound?

4. Think of what will happen in your story. What problem will be solved?

5. What is the beginning? What happens in the middle? How does it end?

6. Share your story with a partner.

▲ Robert Faust and Eugene Friesen. "Voice of the Wood."

 **Art Criticism**

Describe Describe the instrument you chose.

Analyze Is your instrument a string, wind, keyboard, or percussion instrument?

Interpret What feelings do you have when you hear your instrument?

Decide Do you think you succeeded in writing a story about an instrument?

Pattern, Rhythm, and Movement

◀ **John James Audubon.**
(American). *Great Blue Heron.*
1834.

Engraving, aquatint on paper. $37 \frac{1}{2} \times 25 \frac{1}{2}$ inches (95.25 × 64.77 cm.). Orlando Museum of Art, Orlando, Florida.

Artists use pattern, rhythm, and movement to organize elements and objects in works of art.

Artists use **motifs** to create a **pattern** in a work of art.

▶ Artists use **rhythm** in their artwork to create a sense of visual **movement.**

▶ Where do you see patterns on the bird?

▶ Where do you see rhythms?

In This Unit you will learn about pattern, rhythm, and movement and how other artists use these methods in their designs.

Here are the topics you will study.
▶ Pattern and Motif
▶ Regular Patterns
▶ Alternating Patterns
▶ Rhythm
▶ Visual Rhythm
▶ Three-Dimensional Rhythm

John James Audubon

(1785–1851)

John James Audubon, born in Santo Domingo, was known for his fanatical interest in birds and nature. He was a self-taught artist who broke the tradition of painting birds in stiff profile. He was passionate about portraying the distinguishing characteristics of birds. In 1827 he published *Birds of America,* a set of color plates. Color plates were color images put together to create an album. The 435 plates were completed in 1839. The first edition was called the "Elephant Folio," because the album was so big.

Pattern and Motif

Look at the artwork on these pages. *Easy Chair* is made of walnut, maple, and hand stitched upholstery. *White Pine Mosaic* is made with white pine and resin. Both artists have used **motif** and **pattern** in their works of art.

▲ **Philip Moulthrop.** (American). *White Pine Mosaic.* 1993.

9 $\frac{1}{4}$ × 11 $\frac{3}{4}$ × 11 $\frac{3}{4}$ inches (23.50 × 27.95 × 29.85 cm.). Mint Museum of Craft, Charlotte, North Carolina.

 Art History and Culture

Philip Moulthrop believed in creating works of art that displayed the simple shapes and forms found in wood.

◀ **Caleb Gardner.**
(American). *Easy Chair.* 1758.
....
Walnut, maple, and hand stitched upholstery. 46 $\frac{3}{8}$ × 32 $\frac{3}{8}$ × 25 $\frac{7}{8}$ inches (117.8 × 82.2 × 65.7 cm.). The Metropolitan Museum of Art, New York, New York.

Study both pieces of art to discover how artists use pattern and motif.

▶ What shapes are repeated in *Easy Chair*?

▶ What shapes are the motif in *White Pine Mosaic*?

▶ How does the motif change on *Easy Chair*?

Aesthetic Perception

Seeing Like an Artist Think about a tree or plant you have seen. Are all the leaves on the plants or trees exactly the same?

Using Pattern and Motif

People often use patterns to decorate objects.

A **pattern** is a repeated surface decoration. The **motif** is the unit of repetition in the pattern. The motif is made of objects or art elements.

In a **random pattern,** the motif is repeated in no particular order.

In this photograph of leaves, one leaf is the motif. The repetition of the leaves creates a random pattern of leaves.

Practice

Use color, line, and shape to design a motif.

1. Fold your sheet of paper into four sections. Using your pencil, draw a different motif in each section.

2. Using only black and white, draw one motif. Using straight lines, draw a second motif. Use a free-form shape to draw a third motif. In your fourth section, create a motif of your choice. Use colored pencils to complete your motifs.

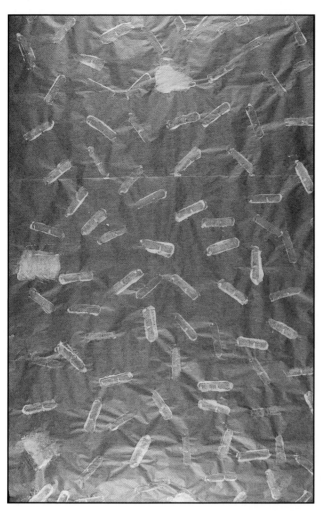

Think about how this student artist used pattern and motif.

◀ **Rosemary Ankerich.**
Age 7.

 Creative Expression

Create a random print, using a potato as a stamp.

1. First cut your potato in half. On the cut side, use the pointed end of a pencil to make a design in the potato.

2. Dip the cut side of the potato into paint.

3. Randomly press the potato onto newspaper or a brown paper bag to create a pattern.

4. Use the paper as wrapping paper for a gift.

 **Art Criticism**

Describe List the steps you followed to create your wrapping paper.

Analyze What is the motif in your pattern?

Interpret What could you wrap with your paper?

Decide If you could redo this design, what shapes would you use?

Regular Patterns

Look at the two works of art on these pages. *Four by Four* is a piece of decorative furniture made of mahogany. *Warnyu (flying foxes)* shows flying foxes in their coops. Each animal is the same, with each head facing the same way. Both works of art show several regular patterns.

◀ **Tom Loeser.** (American).
Four by Four.
• •
Painted mohagany. 44 $\frac{1}{4}$ × 33 $\frac{3}{4}$ × 17 inches
(112.40 × 82.73 × 43.18 cm.). Renwick Gallery,
Smithsonian American Art Museum, Washington, D.C.

 Art History and Culture

What do you think *Four by Four* was used for? Why?

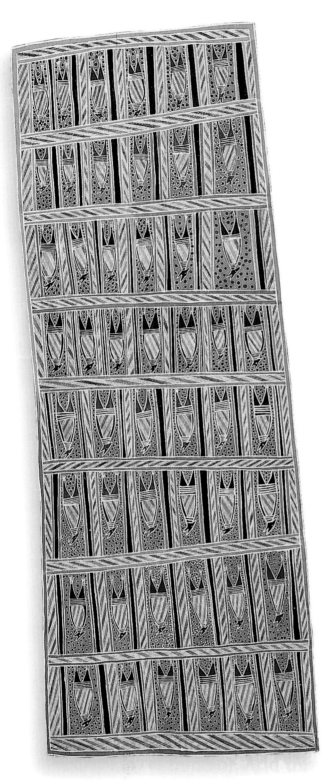

Study both works of art to find the following elements of pattern.

► Which work of art has patterns that are repeated?

► Find the objects that are repeated.

► How are textures used?

◄ **Dorothy Djukulul.**
(Aboriginal/Australia).
Warnyu (flying foxes).
....
1989. Eucalyptus bark. 106.30
× 31.89 inches (270 × 81 cm.).
Kluge-Ruhe Collection of the
University of Virginia,
Charlottesville, Virginia.

 **Aesthetic Perception**

Seeing Like an Artist Look around your classroom at clothes and other fabrics. Find repeated shapes, lines, colors, and textures that are evenly spaced.

Using Regular Patterns

Patterns are surface decorations.

We see patterns on the clothes we wear. Patterns are also used in construction. Patterns are decorative and can be slightly raised.

A **regular pattern** is one kind of decorative surface design.

In a regular pattern the motif, or unit of repetition, is repeated in an even manner.

Look at the drawing to the left. Name the motif. Why is it an example of regular pattern?

Practice

1. Fold a sheet of paper into six equal boxes. In the middle of the first box, draw a large geometric shape, or write large and print a letter of the alphabet.

2. Draw exactly the same motif in each box to create regular pattern. Put equal amounts of space in between each letter or shape.

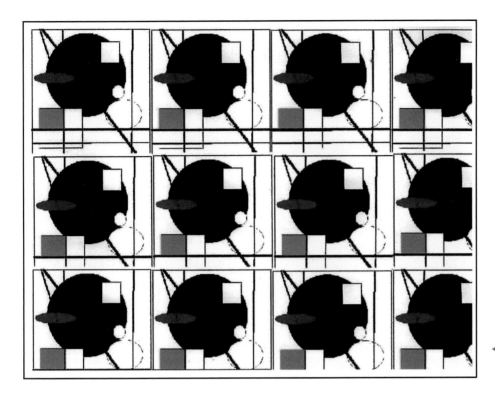

◀ **Carl Blanton.**
Age 8.

Think about how this student used regular pattern in his design.

Creative Expression

Use lines, shapes, and colors to repeat a motif, creating a design.

1. Use the auto-shape tool to create a square.

2. Use the line and auto-shape tools to create a design in the square.

3. Use the fill tool to color in the design.

4. Select the whole design and copy.

5. Paste the design several times to create a regular pattern.

6. Enlarge the completed square design.

7. Print your work.

Art Criticism

Describe What designs did you use to create your motif?

Analyze Which colors did you repeat to create your design?

Interpret How would your designs be different if you did not use the computer?

Decide If you could add one more design, what would it be?

Alternating Patterns

Look at the works of art on these two pages. *Tunic* was made between the fifteenth and sixteenth centuries. A tunic like this was probably a royal gift from the emperor to reward military achievements. *Collar* is a beadwork. It was created in the early 1900s by the Mojave people of the American Southwest region. Both works of art show alternating patterns.

◀ **Artist Unknown.** (Peru). *Tunic.*
Fifteenth–sixteenth century.
....
Camel hair. 37 × 29 inches (93.99 × 73.67 cm.).
The Metropolitan Museum of Art. New York, New York

 Art History and Culture

Do *Tunic* and *Collar* seem to come from the same culture?

▲ **Artist Unknown**.
(Mojave/North
America). *Collar*.
1900–1925.
. . . .
Glass beads and threads.
Birmingham Museum of
Art, Birmingham, Alabama.

Study both works of art to find alternating patterns.

▶ Find the motifs in each work of art.

▶ In which piece is an alternating pattern harder to notice?

▶ Which piece has the most complicated pattern?

Aesthetic Perception

Seeing Like an Artist Look at the artwork in this book to find other examples of alternating patterns.

Using Alternating Patterns

There are many ways to create patterns with one or more motifs. In a random pattern, the **motif,** or unit of repetition, is repeated in no particular order. In a regular pattern, the motif is repeated in an even manner. An **alternating pattern** can use one or more motifs.

Alternating patterns can be created in different ways. Using two repeated motifs that alternate in the same row can create alternating patterns. Changing the position of the motif so that one is upright and the next one is upside down is another way to create an alternating pattern.

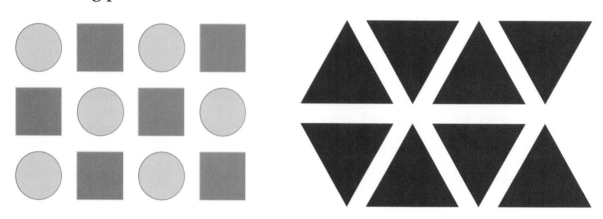

Practice

Alternate a pattern with a group of seven students. Create an alternating pattern while role-playing.

1. Have students stand in a single-file line.

2. One student should stand upright while the next student bends down.

3. Try different ways of creating alternating patterns. What other types of patterns can you create like this?

Think about how this student artist used an alternating pattern.

◄ **Caroline Flynn.**
Age 8.

 **Creative Expression**

Create a motif.

1. Create two motifs that you would wear on a shirt or jacket, such as cars, books, bicycles, or footballs.

2. Draw the article of clothing. Use an alternating pattern of the two motifs you created.

3. Color with crayons.

 **Art Criticism**

Describe What motif did you choose?

Analyze How did you organize your motif into a pattern?

Interpret Where would you wear this shirt?

Decide Did you use an alternating pattern successfully?

Rhythm

▲ **Rosa Bonheur.** (French). *Plowing in Nivernais Region.* 1849.

Oil on canvas. 52 $\frac{1}{2}$ × 102 inches (133.35 × 259.08 cm.). The John and Mable Ringling Museum of Art, Sarasota, Florida.

Look at the works of art on these two pages. In *Plowing in Nivernais Region* the oxen are the beats of the rhythm and the spaces between them rests. *Hannukkah Menorah* is made of stainless steel, silver, and gold. There are three major beats in this sculpture. Each object is a beat, and the spaces between them are the rests.

 Art History and Culture

In 1852 Rosa Bonheur asked for permission to dress in men's clothing in order to attend a horse fair. Women at the time were not allowed into such events.

▲ **Abrasha.** *Hannukkah Menorah.* 1995.

Stainless steel, silver, and gold. $6 \frac{7}{8} \times 17 \frac{1}{4} \times 2 \frac{7}{8}$ inches (17.5 × 43.8 × 9.8 cm.). Renwick Gallery, Smithsonian American Art Museum, Washington, D.C.

Study each work of art to find the following elements of rhythm.

▶ Can you find three major beats in this sculpture?

▶ What other repetitions do you see in the sculpture?

▶ Which work has regular rhythm, and which one has uneven repetitions?

Aesthetic Perception

Seeing Like an Artist Look around the classroom to find objects that are repeated. Do they create any sense of rhythm?

Using Rhythm

Rhythm is a hand-clapping, toe-tapping musical beat. It is created by a beat and a rest between beats.

In visual art, **rhythm** is created by the repetition of a positive shape or form. That object is the beat. The negative space between the repetitions is the **rest.**

Practice

Practice joining pieces of clay. Use slip and scoring.

1. Divide a piece of clay into small balls.

2. Score the edges to be joined with a tool. Brush slip onto one surface.

3. Gently press the two scored surfaces together and smooth over the seam.

◄ **Erica Dazzle Krasle.**
Age 8.

Think about how this student artist created visual rhythm.

 **Creative Expression**

How can you make a useful object that has visual rhythm? Make a clay container to hold different objects.

1. Make three to five pinch pots. The smallest should have a 3-inch opening.

2. Use scoring and slip to join the pots at their sides to make an interesting rhythm of round pots.

3. Smooth the places where they are joined using a clay tool or your fingers.

4. Decorate your bowls by pressing in or adding on patterns using your clay tools or found objects.

Art Criticism

Describe List three steps you followed to create your useful object.

Analyze How did you give your work a rhythmic look?

Interpret What objects would you keep in this container?

Decide Were you successful in creating an object with visual rhythm?

Visual Rhythm

Look at both paintings on these pages. *Parade* shows diagonal movement with the marchers' legs and arms swaying. The movement in *Pueblo Scene Corn Dance, Hopi* appears to be very calm. Both artists used visual rhythm in the design of their works of art.

▲ **Jacob Lawrence.** (American). *Parade.*

1960. Tempera on wood. 23 $\frac{1}{2}$ × 30 $\frac{1}{8}$ inches (58.42 × 76.60 cm.). Hirshhorn Museum, Washington, D.C.

Art History and Culture

Fred Kabotie was a painter, illustrator, and writer of Hopi life, or Nakayoma, which means "day by day."

◀ **Fred Kabotie.**
(Native American).
***Pueblo Scene Corn
Dance, Hopi.*** 1947.
. . . .
Oil on canvas. 29 $\frac{1}{2}$ × 25 $\frac{1}{2}$
inches (74.93 × 64.77 cm.).
Gilcrease Museum, Tulsa,
Oklahoma.

Study each painting to find the following elements.

▶ What are the beats that repeat to create visual
   rhythm?

▶ How does the artist show a sense of calm in
   Pueblo Scene Corn Dance, Hopi?

▶ Which painting shows strong diagonal movement?

▶ Find the colors that are repeated.

Aesthetic Perception

Design Awareness Find examples of rhythm
in your classroom.

Using Visual Rhythm

Visual rhythm is rhythm you see with your eyes. Visual rhythm is the feeling of movement created when an artist repeats colors, shapes, lines, and textures to pull your eyes through a work of art. Your eyes move along the artwork, following the parts that are repeated.

Practice

Demonstrate visual rhythm by creating a design.

1. Cut eight complex geometric shapes out of construction paper.

2. On another piece of construction paper, arrange the shapes to form a design that will create visual rhythm. Use your shapes to create designs that show a sense of calm or movement.

3. Remember that the shapes are *beats* in your design.

◀ **Haley Brennan.**
Age 9.

Think about parades you have seen. What did you like about the parade?

Creative Expression

1. Think about things you like to see in a parade. Do you like floats, marching bands, clowns, horses, elephants, and antique cars?

2. Make sketches of things you want in your parade. Draw yourself as the grand marshal or leader of the parade.

3. Select your best sketches and use chalk to transfer them to large paper.

4. Paint your parade.

Art Criticism

Describe What did you include in your parade?

Analyze How did you create rhythm in your picture?

Interpret What is the occasion or holiday for your parade?

Decide Were you successful in creating visual rhythm?

Three-Dimensional Rhythm

◄ **John Hoover.** (American).
Looner Eclipse. 1999.

Cedar. 40 × 48 inches (101.6 × 121.92 cm.).
Private Collection.

Look at the works of art on these pages. *Looner Eclipse* shows birds sitting on the moon, pushing it down. The four birds across the top of the moon create rhythm. *Case with Five Baluster* shows jumbled repetitions of triangles, rectangles, circles, and curves. If you could hear this work, it would have three movements. Both artists have used three-dimensional rhythm in their works of art.

 Art History and Culture

John Hoover, a native of Alaska, created a sculpture about the legends and stories of the native people of Alaska.

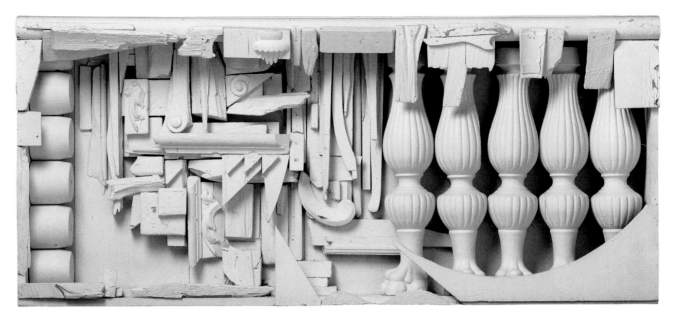

Study both works of art. How did the artists use rhythm in their works of art?

▶ How did the artists create rhythm?

▶ Describe the shapes that are repeated.

▶ Which artwork uses a variety of different shapes?

▲ **Louise Nevelson.** (American). *Case with Five Baluster.* 1959.

Painted wood. 27 $\frac{5}{8}$ × 63 $\frac{5}{8}$ × 9 $\frac{1}{2}$ inches (68.58 × 160.02 × 24.13 cm.). Walker Art Center, Minneapolis, Minnesota.

Aesthetic Perception

Design Awareness Look around the classroom to see different shapes that repeat.

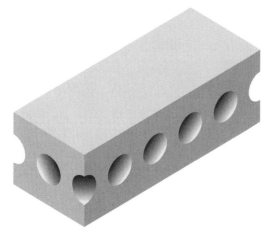

Using Three-Dimensional Rhythm

Three-dimensional rhythm is a principle of design that indicates movement by the repetition of elements in a form.

In three-dimensional art there are different ways an artist can create rhythm. One way is by repeating several negative spaces in a work where a number of holes are carved into it. Another way is by organizing and repeating similar forms, or by repeating textures on forms such as hair texture or fur texture.

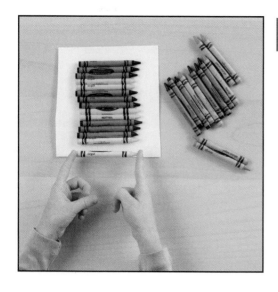

Practice

In groups of five, role-play to create a sense of rhythm.

1. Look around the classroom for three-dimensional materials, such as books on the shelf.

2. In small groups, experiment with the objects to find rhythmic patterns.

3. Place the objects in such a way that the rest of the class can identify the rhythmic pattern.

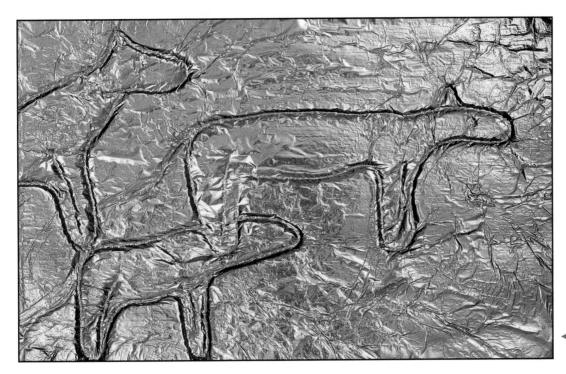

◄ **Leah Goode.**
Age 8.

Think about how the student artist used three-dimensional rhythm.

 **Creative Expression**

How can you create a relief sculpture of repeating animal forms?

1. Think about an animal you would like to use. Look at pictures of that animal.

2. Make sketches of the animal. Select your best sketches and draw the animal several times on the cardboard to create a rhythmic repetition of the animal.

3. Glue yarn over the outlines of your animals.

4. Cover the surface with aluminum foil. Start pressing foil near the center. As you work, gently press the foil around each raised line with your fingertips.

Art Criticism

Describe What animals did you choose for your artwork?

Analyze Describe the rhythm of the animals in your artwork.

Interpret Give your work an expressive title.

Decide Were you successful in creating an animal relief design?

Pattern, Rhythm, and Movement

▲ **Mir Sayyid 'Ali.** (Persian). *Nighttime in a Palace.* c. 1539–1543.

Opaque watercolor, gold, and silver on paper. 11.26 × 7.87 inches (28.6 × 20 cm.). Arthur M. Sackler Museum, Harvard University, Cambridge, Massachusetts.

 **Art Criticism** **Critical Thinking**

Describe What do you see?

Describe the people. What are they wearing and what are they doing?

▶ What animals do you see?

Analyze How is this work organized?

Where do you see patterns?

▶ Where do you see regular patterns?

▶ Where do you see alternating patterns?

Interpret What is the artist trying to say?

What do you think is happening in this painting?

▶ Does one person seem to stand out?

▶ Look at the upper-left corner. Who do you think the elderly couple is?

▶ Is this a calm or active painting? Explain.

Decide What do you think about the work?

Is the work successful because it is realistic, well organized, or because it has a strong message? Explain.

Pattern, Rhythm, and Movement, continued

Show What You Know

Answer these questions on a separate sheet of paper.

1 A motif is used to create a _____.
  A. pattern
  B. rhythm
  C. movement

2 _____ has a beat—the positive shape or form—and a rest—the negative space between the beats.
  A. Visual rhythm
  B. Pattern
  C. Flowing rhythm

3 In _____ rhythm, there are no sudden changes in line or breaks in movement.
  A. movement
  B. flowing
  C. visual

4 The repetition of a motif with equal amounts of space between is a/an _____.
  A. alternating pattern
  B. random pattern
  C. regular pattern

5 Repeating motifs with changes in position or content are _____.
  A. alternating patterns
  B. alternating motifs
  C. motifs

CAREERS IN ART
Graphic Design

Graphic Designers design magazines, ads, and promotional material. The job requires familiarity with type, color, and layout.

Audio Visual Designers develop slide presentations from a series of drawings and collages given to them by clients. A script and soundtrack are added to complete the presentation. This talent for balancing imagery and sound makes audio visual designers an important part of the presentation process.

▲ **Graphic Designer**

Pattern, Rhythm, and Movement in Dance

▲ African American Dance ensemble. "Isicathulo."

Isicathulo is a Zulu step dance from South Africa. Zulu dockworkers and gold miners perform clever, syncopated routines accompanied by a guitar and whistle. They create rhythmic dances by organizing their well-rehearsed patterns of movement.

What to Do Make rhythmic patterns of sounds that can be organized different ways to create dances.

1. Create a rhythmic movement that can be repeated. Include slapping your legs, stomping your feet, snapping your fingers, clapping, or hopping. Give your pattern a name.

2. Form groups of three students. Each person shares one pattern and teaches it to the others.

3. Practice all the patterns in a line formation, either shoulder-to-shoulder or in single-file, and perform in unison.

4. Choose a leader to call out the name of each pattern to be performed.

 **Art Criticism**

Describe What pattern names did your group learn?

Analyze Does the name of each pattern provide a clue for the movement?

Interpret Did the rhythmic patterns "feel" right? Did you change them to work better?

Decide Were you successful in making the rhythm and movements work together?

Harmony, Variety, Emphasis, and Unity

Artists create harmony, variety, emphasis, and unity in their works of art.

Frederic Remington's use of line, color, and texture created harmony, variety, emphasis, and unity in this form.

◀ **Frederic Remington.** (American). *Mountain Man.* 1903.

Bronze. The Carleton Collection.

Artists use **harmony** to make works of art look pleasing or peaceful.

▶ Where do you see lines in *Mountain Man* that are similar?

Artists use **variety** to create interest.

▶ Describe at least two different textures that you see.

Artists use **emphasis** to create a center of interest in their works.

▶ Which part of the artwork draws your attention most?

Harmony and variety create a feeling of **unity** in an artwork.

▶ What unifies this sculpture?

In This Unit you will learn and practice techniques for creating harmony, variety, and emphasis. You will also learn how harmony and variety create a feeling of unity.

Here are the topics you will study:
▶ Harmony
▶ Variety
▶ Emphasis
▶ Unity

Self-Portrait on a Horse.

Frederic Remington
(1861–1909)

Frederic Remington was born in Canton, New York, on October 1, 1861. As a young boy, he loved to draw Native Americans, cowboys, soldiers, and horses. When he was 19 years old, he left college and traveled west. He spent four years as a cowboy and a rancher and sketched everything he saw. His artwork focuses on the American West.

Harmony

Look at the containers on these pages. The *Jar* was created in Japan more than 4,000 years ago. The *Pottery Vessels* were crafted by Nancy Youngblood in the 1980s. All the containers were made with clay. These works contain repeated lines and textures that create harmony.

◀ **Artist Unknown.** (Japan).
Jar. Middle Jomon period.
c. 3000–2000 B.C.
••••••••••••••••••••••••••••••••
Earthenware clay with applied, incised, and cord-marked decoration. 27 $\frac{1}{2}$ inches high (69.85 cm.). The Metropolitan Museum of Art, New York, New York.

 Art History and Culture

How do you think these containers could have been used in everyday life?

◄ **Nancy Youngblood.** (Pueblo, United States). *Pottery Vessels.* 1980–1985.

Pottery. 4 $\frac{1}{2}$ × 6 inches (11.43 × 15.24 cm.). Courtesy Nancy Youngblood.

Study each ceramic piece to find examples of visual harmony.

- ▶ Which shapes are repeated?
- ▶ Which textures are repeated?
- ▶ Locate one of the motifs in each piece.
- ▶ Where do you see lines that are repeated?

Aesthetic Perception

Seeing Like an Artist Find a work of art in this book that seems peaceful to you. Which shapes, lines, or colors are repeated in it?

Using Harmony

Harmony is the peaceful look made when related elements of art are put together. Visual artists can create harmony by repeating lines, colors, shapes, textures, and objects.

Harmony can be created with colors that are related on the color wheel.

Harmony can be created with similar shapes.

Harmony can be created with similar lines.

 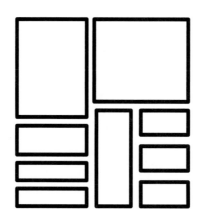 

Practice

Create harmony with color, shape, and repetition.

1. Fold a sheet of paper into three parts. Draw a simple shape in the first part using markers or crayons. Color it with three related colors.

2. In the second part, draw a geometric shape. Repeat the shape in different sizes until this part is filled.

3. In the last part, draw rows of repeating lines and shapes.

◀ **Chandler Hogan.**
Age 7.
◀ **Spencer Hanson.**
Age 7.

Think about how these student artists created harmony in their clay bowls.

🎨 Creative Expression

Whom do you admire? Create a figural clay bowl to honor someone you admire. Use color to create harmony in your bowl.

1. Begin by making a pinch pot. Then roll a coil to make arms that will fit halfway around the rim of your pot. Roll a sphere to make a head.

2. Using proper joining techniques, attach the arms and head to the rim of your pot. Add clay for hair. With your clay tools add details such as hands, eyes, and a mouth. Add texture to the hair.

3. Choose related colors to paint or glaze your figural pot once it has been fired.

❗ Art Criticism

Describe Describe the steps taken to create your clay bowl.

Analyze How did you create harmony in your bowl?

Interpret How does your clay bowl represent the person you admire?

Decide What would you change if you did this project again?

Variety

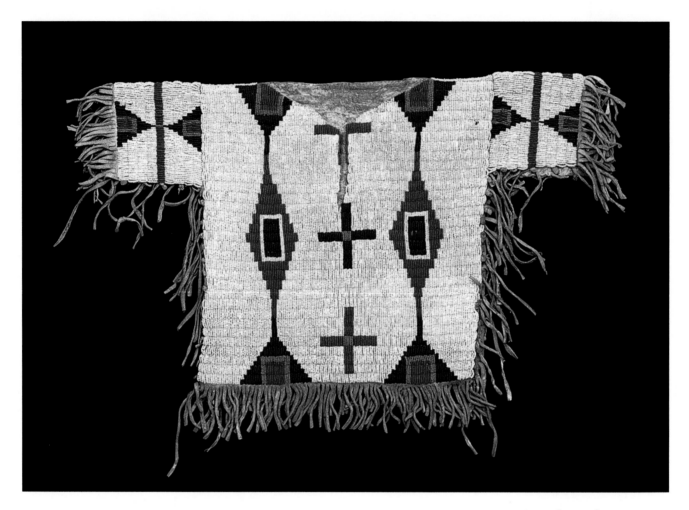

 Look at the textile art on these pages. A Central Plains woman made *Child's Beaded Shirt* around 1865. It is decorated with a variety of textures, colors, and materials. Navajo artist Isabel John created *Pictorial Tapestry* more than 100 years later with a variety of shapes and colors. Both artists used variety in their designs to create interest.

▲ **Artist Unknown.** (Northern Cheyenne or Teton Dakota, United States). *Child's Beaded Shirt.* c. 1865.

Buffalo hide, glass seed beads. 13 $\frac{3}{16}$ × 23 inches (33.5 × 58.5 cm.). Dallas Museum of Art, Dallas, Texas.

Art History and Culture

Compare the materials used to make each work of art. Why do you think the artists chose these materials?

Study both works of art to find examples of variety.

▶ Find different geometric and free-form shapes in the same artwork.

▶ Find shapes of different sizes in each piece.

▶ Locate places where you see different textures.

▶ Which work seems to have more variety?

▲ **Isabel John.** (Navajo, United States). *Pictorial Tapestry.* Mid-1980s.

. . . .

Wool, commercial, and natural dyes. 44 × 77 $\frac{1}{2}$ inches (111.76 × 196.85 cm.). Birmingham Museum of Art, Birmingham, Alabama.

Aesthetic Perception

Seeing Like an Artist Choose an element of art, such as line, color, shape, or texture. How many different varieties can you find in your classroom?

Using Variety

Variety is using different lines, shapes, colors, and textures to make a work of art interesting.

Too much of the same color, line, or shape in an artwork can be boring. Adding something different or unexpected can break up the repetition. Using a variety of colors or lines can give people more to think about.

What has been changed to add variety to the designs below?

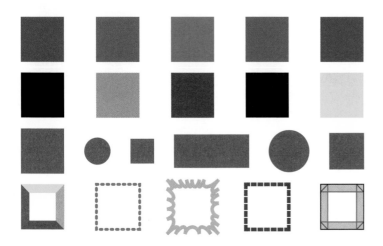

Practice

Create a design that has variety. Use pencil and one other medium.

1. Draw a geometric or free-form shape on your paper with a pencil. Repeat the shape in the same size until your paper is filled.

2. Add a different element to your design to create variety. For example, you might add different colors, lines, or textures.

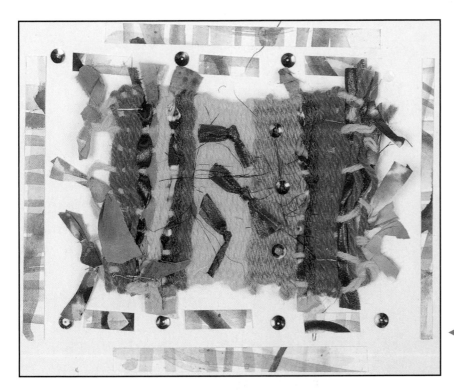

◀ **Joseph Fernandez.** Age 9.

Think about how this student created variety in his weaving.

Creative Expression

What different ways can you use a weaving? Make a weaving with a variety of colors and textures.

1. Think about how you will use your weaving. Select a variety of ribbons, natural fibers, and yarn for your weaving.

2. Cut out a piece of cardboard, and notch it on the top and the bottom. Then, string the warp thread on it.

3. Weave your fibers to create variety.

Art Criticism

Describe What materials did you use in your weaving?

Analyze Which colors and textures did you repeat? Where did you create variety?

Interpret How would the interest of your weaving change if you had used only one color and one texture?

Decide If you could add other colors and textures, what would you choose?

Emphasis

Look at the works of art on these pages. Both are oil paintings. *Hairdresser's Window* is a genre painting. It shows a scene of American life from the time it was painted. *Jane's Remington* is a still life. It shows an inanimate object. Each painting has an area of emphasis.

◀ **John Sloan.** (American). *Hairdresser's Window.* 1907.
Oil on canvas. 32 × 25 $\frac{1}{8}$ inches (81 × 66 cm.). Wadsworth Atheneum Museum of Art, Hartford, Connecticut.

 Art History and Culture

Works of art can be a record of history. What does each of these paintings show about the past?

◀ **Robert Cottingham.** (American). *Jane's Remington.* 2000.

Oil on canvas. 84 × 74 inches (213.36 × 187.96 cm.). Forum Gallery, New York, New York.

Study the works of art to find the areas of emphasis.

▶ Which people and objects do you see in the paintings?

▶ How are the people and objects arranged?

▶ What part of each picture attracts your eye?

Aesthetic Perception

Design Awareness If important information is on the board, what can your teacher do to draw attention to it?

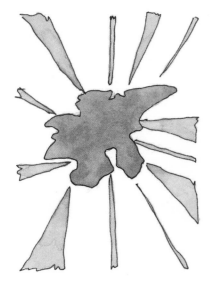

Using Emphasis

Sometimes an artist wants you to look immediately at a certain area in a work of art. This area is the center of interest, or the **focal point.** An artist uses **emphasis** to draw your attention there. Emphasis makes a part of an artwork stand out.

One way to create emphasis is to have everyone in the picture look at one person or thing, like in *Hairdresser's Window.* That becomes the focal point.

Another way to create emphasis in a design is to have lines lead the viewer's eyes to the focal point, as in *Jane's Remington.*

A third way to create emphasis is to use **contrast.** Artists create contrast by making one object different from the rest of the artwork. A bright color stands out from dark colors. A rough texture stands out from a smooth texture.

Practice

Contrast values to create emphasis. Use pencil and black crayon.

1. Draw a shape several times until a small piece of paper is filled. Keep the shapes about the same size.

2. Pick one to be the center of interest. Color it with black crayon, leaving the rest of the shapes uncolored to create emphasis.

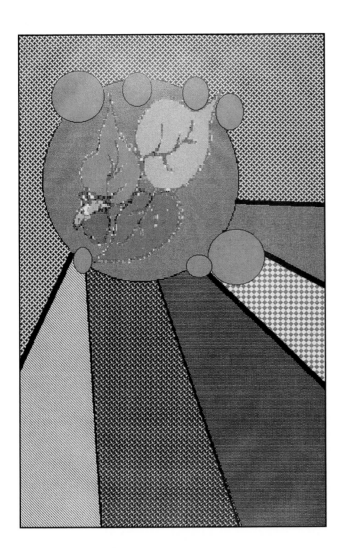

Think about how this student created an area of emphasis.

◀ **Carl Blanton.**
Age 8.

Creative Expression

What object in nature would you like to emphasize? Make a computer design with that object as the focal point.

1. Use the ellipse tool to draw a circle. Use the draw tool to draw something from nature within the circle.

2. Use the line tool to draw diagonal lines that connect to the circle. Use the fill tool to fill the sections around the circle with shades of gray.

3. Use the brush tool to paint the design inside the circle. Make it colorful.

Art Criticism

Describe List the procedures you used to make this work.

Analyze How did you create a focal point?

Interpret Give your work a creative title.

Decide Were you successful in creating a design with emphasis?

Emphasis Through Decoration

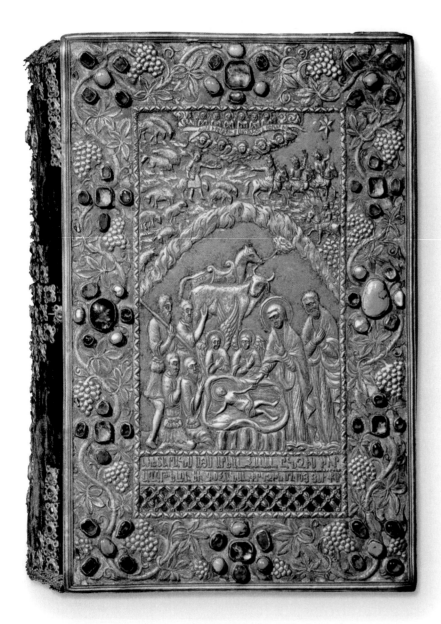

◄ **Artist Unknown.** (Armenia).
Cover of Armenian Book.
Thirteenth century.
....
Carved and hammered silver, gilded and
enameled, and set with jewels, and rubricated
vellum. 10 $\frac{1}{4}$ × 7 $\frac{3}{8}$ × inches (26.04 × 18.73 cm.).
The Metropolitan Museum of Art, New York,
New York.

Look at the books on these pages. *Cover of Armenian Book* was made by hand during the thirteenth century. The pages of the book contain prayers and illustrations. *British Museum Memoir* was also made by hand about 700 years later. The pages contain private writings and drawings. Each artist decorated the cover to create emphasis.

 Art History and Culture

Whom do you think owned the *Cover of Armenian Book*?
Why?

▲ **Pamela Spitzmueller.**
(American). *British Museum Memoir.* 1997.

Small grid graph paper, colored pencil, copper sheet, and copper wire. 11 × 47 inches (27.94 × 119.38 cm.). National Museum of Women in the Arts, Washington, D.C.

Study the books to find examples of emphasis.

▶ Which colors and textures do you see in each work?

▶ What part of *British Museum Memoir* draws your attention first?

▶ What do you think the artist felt was the most important area of *Cover of Armenian Book*?

Aesthetic Perception

Design Awareness Have you ever chosen a book just because you liked the cover? What about the cover drew you to it?

Using Emphasis Through Decoration

When you add decoration to one area of an otherwise plain design, you emphasize that area of the design.

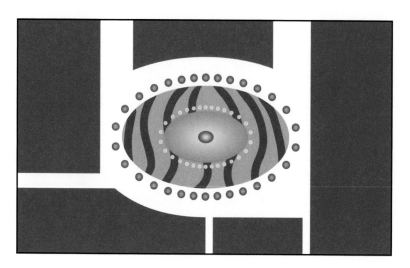

Practice

Create emphasis in a drawing of your favorite activity.

1. Think of an activity you like to do, such as roller skating, painting, or playing an instrument. Draw a sketch of yourself doing your favorite activity. Draw the background.

2. Color just you doing the activity. Leave the rest of the drawing plain.

3. Do you look like the most important thing in your drawing?

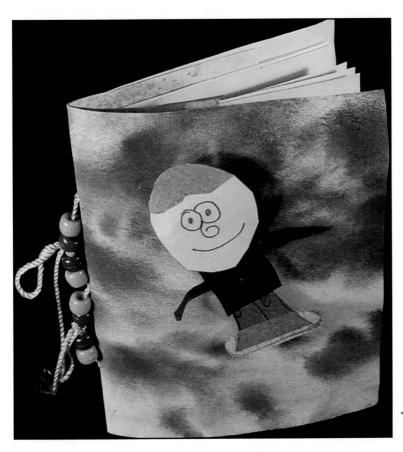

Think about how this student created emphasis on his book cover.

◀ **Josh Nelms.**
Age 9.

 Creative Expression

Can you create a book using emphasis on your cover?

1. Use a sheet of paper for the cover. Use a wash of warm or cool colors on the sheet. Let it dry.

2. On a sheet of construction paper, re-create your drawing from the Practice activity. Cut the image out. Glue a paper ring to the back.

3. Stack three sheets of paper on top of your cover. Fold it in half so that the cover is on the outside. Stitch your pages together. Glue the paper ring to the cover so the image is raised from the surface.

 **Art Criticism**

Describe What activity did you portray yourself doing?

Analyze Which contrasting colors did you use for your cover? How did you create emphasis?

Interpret If you had to put a title on your book cover, what would it be?

Decide What would you change if you did this project again?

Unity Through Color

Look at the works of art on these pages. Andy Warhol made a series of silkscreens of these flowers. Each print was painted in different colors. The fish in *Gin Matsuba* is a type of Japanese fish called koi. Lundin Kudo makes sculptures of koi. Each artist used one color throughout these works of art.

◀ **Andy Warhol.** (American). *Flowers.* 1967.

Silk screen ink and synthetic polymer paint on canvas. $115\frac{1}{2} \times 115\frac{1}{2}$ inches (293.4×293.4 cm.). Museum of Contemporary Art, San Diego, California.

 Art History and Culture

Koi are like a living work of art! They are popular ornamental pond fish that are sometimes called "living jewels" or "swimming flowers."

▲ **Lundin Kudo.**
(American).
Gin Matsuba.
....
19 × 7 × 9 inches (48.26
× 17.78 × 22.86 cm.).
Private Collection.

Study the works of art to find unity.

▶ Which repeated shapes create harmony in
   Flowers?

▶ Which different lines and textures create variety in
   Gin Matsuba?

▶ What colors do you see in each work of art?

Aesthetic Perception

Seeing Like an Artist Where do you see examples of unity
in your classroom?

Using Unity

Unity is the "invisible glue" that makes different parts look as if they belong together. It helps you see a work of art as a whole instead of as separate parts.

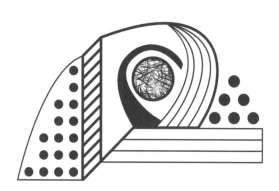

Harmony is created by using similar lines, shapes, colors, or textures. Variety is created by using different lines, shapes, colors, or textures. Works of art that have harmony or variety can also have unity. One way an artist can create unity is by making everything in a work one color, texture, or shape. This is called **simplicity.**

Practice

Create and color a design that illustrates unity. Use a crayon.

1. Draw a variety of geometric and free-form shapes to create a design.

2. Color all of the shapes with the same color.

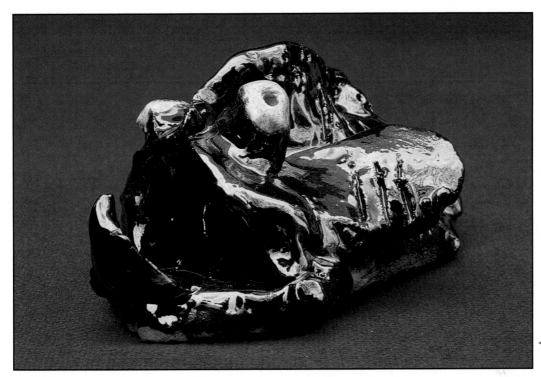

Think about how this student created unity in his fish.

Creative Expression

Have you ever seen a fish with interesting textures on its body? Create a clay fish with unity.

1. Flatten a palm-sized ball of clay until it is about as thick as your little finger. Fold the clay like a taco. Score the edges and seal it along the top.

2. Shape clay into fins and eyes. Attach by scoring, applying slip, and smoothing. Pinch a tail.

3. Use clay tools to create scales. Make interesting textures on your fish.

4. After the fish is fired, glaze or paint it with one color.

Art Criticism

Describe List the steps you followed to create your clay fish.

Analyze How did you give your work a variety of textures? How did you create unity?

Interpret Give your clay fish a name that sums up its expressive quality.

Decide Were you able to successfully create unity in your ceramic sculpture?

Unity, Repetition, and Grouping

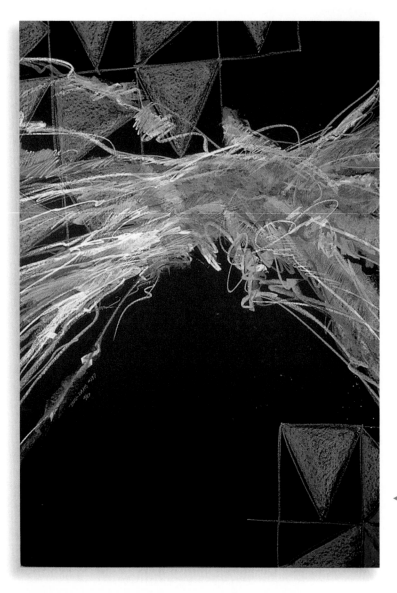

Look at the paintings on these pages. Henri Matisse painted *Woman in Blue* in France. About 50 years later, Willis "Bing Davis" painted *Ancestral Spirit Dance Series,* an abstract design based on memories of African dancers. Both artists have created unity to give their work a feeling of wholeness.

◀ **Willis "Bing" Davis.** (American). *Ancestral Spirit Dance Series.* 1990.

Oil pastel. 60 × 40 inches (152.4 × 101.6 cm.). Collection of Willis Bing Davis.

 Art History and Culture

Why do you think the artists created these works of art?

Study both works of art to find examples of unity.

▶ Where do you see geometric shapes combined with wild zigzag lines?

▶ Name the colors in each work. How many are there in each?

▶ Locate the thin lines repeated throughout *Woman in Blue.*

◀ **Henri Matisse.** (French). *Woman in Blue.* 1937.

Oil on canvas. 36½ × 29 inches (92.71 × 73.66 cm.). Philadelphia Museum of Art, Philadelphia, Pennsylvania.

Aesthetic Perception

Seeing Like an Artist Look outdoors. Find objects in nature that are surrounded by a single color.

Using Repetition and Grouping to Create Unity

Unity is the feeling of wholeness in a work of art. Artists use repetition and grouping to show that different parts of a work belong together.

Repetition is when an artist repeats lines, shapes, colors, or textures. An architect, for example, might repeat colors and textures on the outside of a house.

Objects that are grouped together are unified by what surrounds them. Seashells arranged on a beach are a good example of unity. They are usually different shapes and sizes, but the sand in the background unifies them.

Practice

Illustrate unity. Use pencil and crayon.

1. Draw a large free-form shape. Fill it with a variety of smaller geometric shapes.

2. Use pencil to darken the spaces between the geometric shapes. Use crayon to color the whole area outside the free-form shape one color.

◀ **Toni Thompson.**
Age 8.

Think about how this student showed unity in her design.

 **Creative Expression**

How can you use creatures to show unity? Create a crayon engraving.

1. Use crayons to cover a sheet of paper with many different colors. Then, paint the whole surface with thinned black ink until you can no longer see the color.

2. While the ink is drying, sketch a few creatures on scratch paper. Choose some to draw.

3. Engrave the creatures by scratching lines and line patterns in the black background with the pointed end of a paper clip. Add detail and texture.

 **Art Criticism**

Describe What creatures did you draw?

Analyze How did you create unity in your engraving?

Interpret How would the mood of your picture change if you had not covered the surface with black ink?

Decide Can you think of another theme to use for this art project?

Harmony, Variety, Emphasis, and Unity

▲ **Faith Ringgold.** (American). *The Sunflower
Quilting Bee at Arles.* 1991.

Acrylic on canvas, printed and tie-dyed fabric. 74 × 80 inches
(187.96 × 203.2 cm.). Private Collection.

Art Criticism Critical Thinking

Describe What do you see?

During this step you will collect information about the work.

▶ What does the credit line tell us about this work?

▶ Describe the people.

Analyze How is this work organized?

Think about how the artist has used the elements and principles of art.

▶ Where do you see harmony created by similar colors and shapes?

▶ Where do you see variety created by difference?

Interpret What is the artist trying to say?

Use the clues you discovered during your analysis to find the message the artist is trying to show.

▶ What do you think the women are talking about?

▶ Why do you think van Gogh is in the painting?

Decide What do you think about the work?

Use all the information you have gathered to decide whether this is a successful work of art.

▶ Is the work successful because it is realistic, because it is well-organized, or because it has a strong message?

Show What You Know

Answer these questions on a separate sheet of paper.

1 _____ is using different lines, shapes, colors, and textures to make a work look interesting.
A. Harmony
B. Variety
C. Focal point

2 Artists create _____ to make an object look different from the rest of an artwork.
A. contrast
B. unity
C. harmony

3 _____ is the peaceful look made when related elements of art are put together.
A. Harmony
B. Variety
C. Emphasis

4 Which is not an example of unity?
A. Simplicity
B. Grouping
C. Contrast

5 An artist uses emphasis to draw your attention to the _____.
A. repetition
B. focal point
C. unity

VISIT A MUSEUM
The Philadelphia Museum of Art

The Philadelphia Museum of Art was established in Philadelphia, Pennsylvania, in 1875. There are over 300,000 objects in the museum's collection. The Asian collection has artwork dating from 500 B.C. to the present. The European collections have sculpture, stained glass, and paintings. The American collections have paintings, furniture, silver, and Pennsylvania German art. In addition, the museum offers many programs for people of all ages. These include school tours, workshops, and performances for families.

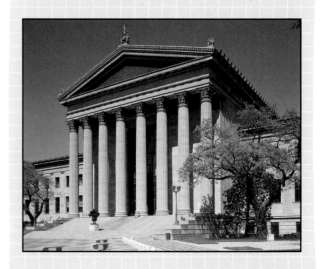

Harmony, Variety, Emphasis, and Unity in Dance

▲ Eugene Loring. "Billy the Kid."

This is a photo of a dancer playing a famous outlaw named "Billy the Kid." The ballet about his life and the Westward Movement shows the chores pioneers did to survive. It was choreographed by Eugene Loring. Aaron Copland composed the music with musical themes based on old cowboy songs.

What to Do Create a dance or mime showing a variety of pioneer work movements.

1. Select a few ideas to show. Some choices include chopping wood or pushing a plow. Experiment by exaggerating the movement and giving it a rhythm.

2. Find three ways to vary each work action. Suggestions are changing the direction or doing it in slow motion.

3. Select two different actions and build a mime or movement sequence.

4. Share with a partner. Combine all four ideas and show a perspective of pioneer work life as you perform them together.

Art Criticism

Describe Describe the way you and your partner worked together.

Analyze What things did you do to create harmony, variety, emphasis, and unity?

Interpret How did it feel to perform the work of pioneers?

Decide Were you successful in creating a pioneer work dance or mime?

Technique Tips
Drawing

Pencil Basics

For darker values, use the side of your pencil lead, press harder, and go over areas more than once. You can add form to your objects using shading.

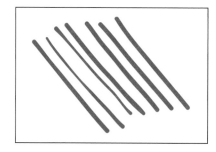

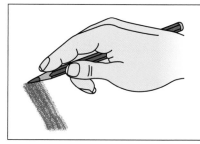

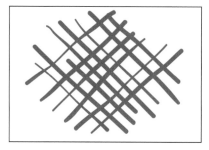

Colored Pencils

You can blend colors with colored pencils. Color with the lighter hue first. Gently go over the light hue with the darker hue until you get the hue you want.

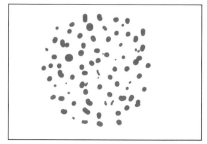

You can create shadows by blending complementary colors.

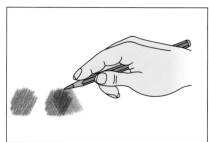

Technique Tips

Crayon Basics

Crayons can be used to make thick and thin lines and dots. You can use both ends of a crayon.

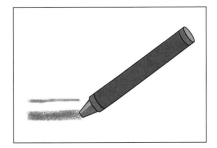

You can color in large areas by using the long side of a crayon.

Marker Basics

You can use the point of a marker to create thin lines and small dots.

You can use the side of a marker tip to make thick lines.

Always replace the cap of a marker when you are finished using it.

Technique Tips

Oil Pastels

Oil pastels can be used like crayons. When you press down hard on oil pastels, your picture will look painted. Oil pastels are soft and break easily. They can also be messy. Wash your hands with soap and water after using them.

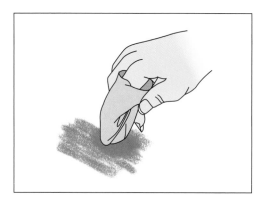

Colors can be mixed or blended by smearing them using a tissue or your finger.

You can use oil pastels to draw over other media, such as tempera and crayon.

Colored Chalk

Colored chalks can be used to make colorful, soft designs. Colored chalk is soft and breaks easily. Reuse broken pieces.

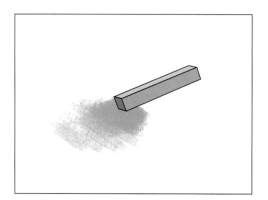

Make bolder colors by going over an area more than once.

Blend colors by using a soft tissue or your finger.

Technique Tips

Painting

Brush Care

Rinse your brush in water between colors.
Blot the brush dry on a paper towel.

Clean the brush when you are finished painting.

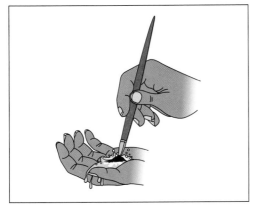

1. Rinse the brush in clean water. Wash the brush with soap.

2. Rinse the brush well again and blot it dry.

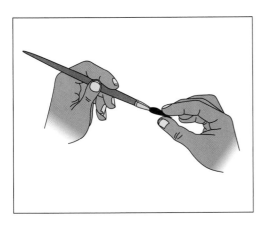

3. Shape the bristles.

4. Store brushes with bristles up.

Technique Tips

Tempera

Wet your brush in a water container. Wipe off extra water using the inside wall of the container and blot the brush on a paper towel.

Mix colors on a palette. Put some of each color that you want to mix on the palette. Add darker colors a little at a time to lighter colors. To create a tint, mix a small amount of a hue into white. To create a shade, mix a small amount of black into a hue.

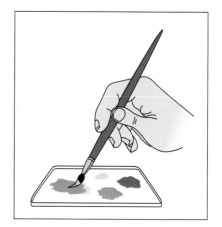

Use a thin, pointed brush to paint thin lines and details.

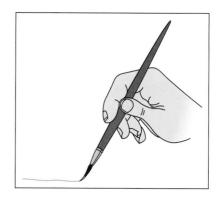

Use a wide brush to paint large areas.

Technique Tips

Watercolors

Wet your brush in a water container. Wipe off extra water using the inside wall of the container and blot the brush on a paper towel. Add a drop of water to each watercolor cake. Rinse your brush between colors.

Mix colors on a palette. Put some of each color that you want to mix on the palette. Add darker colors a little at a time to lighter colors. To create a tint, add more water to a hue. To create a shade, mix a small amount of black into a hue.

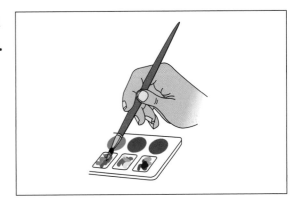

Paint on damp paper to create soft lines and edges. Tape your paper to the table, brush clean water over the paper, and allow the water to soak in.

Paint on dry paper and use very little water to create sharp lines and shapes.

Technique Tips

Watercolor Resists

Certain materials will show through water-colors. Crayons and oil pastels both show through watercolors. To make a watercolor resist, make a drawing using crayons or oil pastels. Then paint over the drawing using watercolors. The watercolors will cover the blank parts of the paper. The watercolors will not be visible on the parts of the paper covered with crayon or oil pastels.

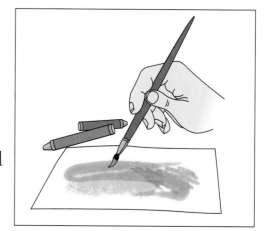

Collage

Scissors

Always cut away from your body.

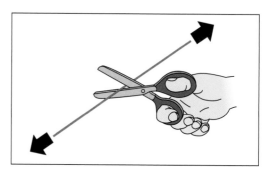

Ask a classmate to stretch yarn or fabric as you cut.

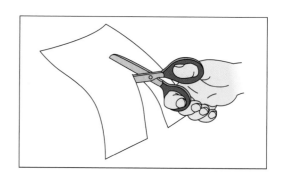

Use folded paper to cut symmetrical shapes. Fold a sheet of paper in half. Cut a shape using the folded edge as the axis.

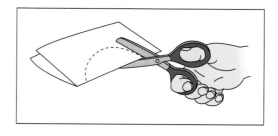

Technique Tips

Arranging a Design

When creating a collage, it is important to plan your design. Take into consideration the size of shapes and spaces, placement of shapes and spaces, color schemes, and textures. When you have made an arrangement you like, glue the shapes in place.

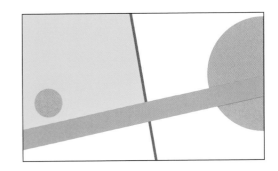

Glue

Squeeze a line of glue onto the paper. You can smooth the line with the tip of the glue bottle.

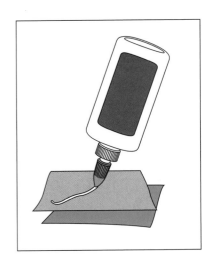

Close the glue bottle and clean the top when you are finished using it.

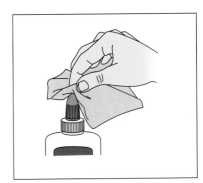

Technique Tips

Texture Rubbing

Place a texture plate or textured surface underneath your paper.

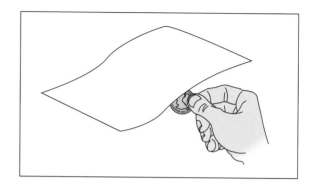

Hold the paper and object down firmly so they do not slip.

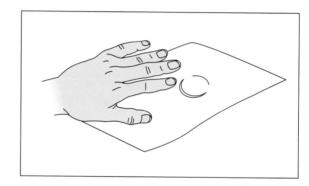

Use the long side of your crayon and rub away from you only. Do not move the crayon back and forth.

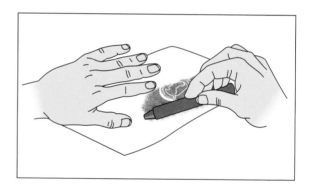

Technique Tips

Printmaking
Making Stamps

You can cut sponges into shapes to make stamps.

You can carve shapes into potatoes to make stamps.

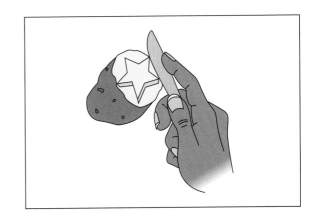

Making a Sponge Print

Use a different sponge for each color. Dip a sponge into paint. Press the sponge onto paper.

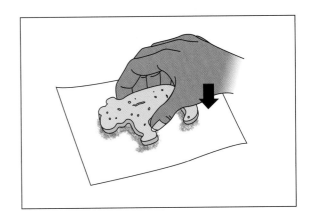

Technique Tips

Printing Stamps

Put a small amount of ink or paint on a flat solid surface. Roll a brayer back and forth in the ink until there is an even coating of ink on the surface and the brayer.

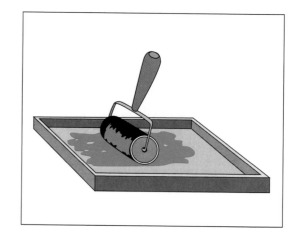

Roll the brayer over your stamp.

Apply the stamp carefully to your paper.

Technique Tips

Sculpture

Clay Basics

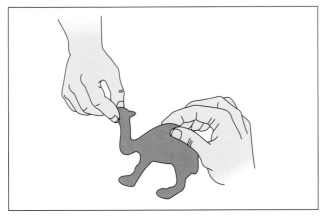

Clay can be pinched, pulled, and squeezed into the desired shape.

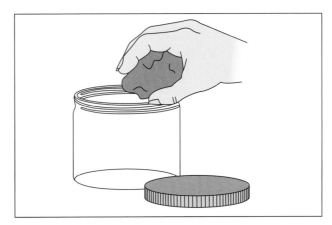

Store clay in an airtight container to keep it from drying out.

Pinch Pots

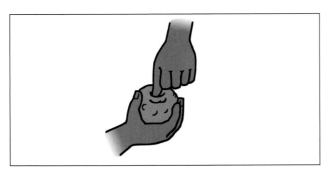

Push your thumb into your clay up to the first joint. Turn the clay on your thumb to create an opening.

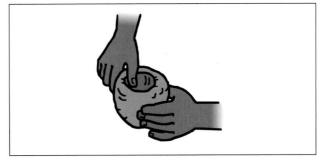

Keeping your thumb in the hole, place your fingers on the outside of the clay and gently squeeze as you turn. Repeat until you have formed a bowl.

Gently tap the bottom of your bowl on your table so that it sits flat.

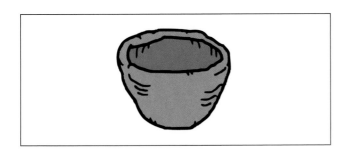

Technique Tips

Joining Clay

Two pieces of clay can be joined together by using slip and scoring.

Score both pieces to help them stick together.

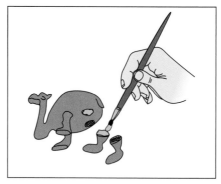

Apply slip to one of the pieces using a brush.

Squeeze together the two pieces of clay. Smooth the edges where they are joined.

Painting Clay

Clay can be painted and decorated with glazes once it is dry or fired.

Technique Tips

Paper Sculpture

You can curl, fold, and bend paper strips to make paper sculptures.

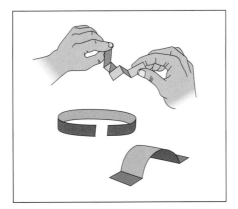

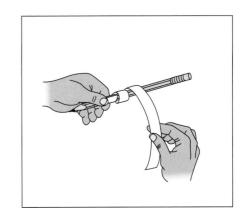

Papier-Mâché

Create a supporting form, if needed. Forms can be made of almost anything. Masking tape can be used to hold the form together.

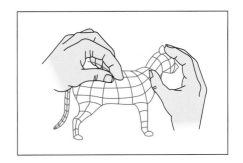

Tear paper into strips. Dip the strips into paste, or rub the paste onto the strips using your fingers. Use wide strips for wide forms and small strips for small forms.

Apply several layers of strips, applying each layer in a different direction. Smooth over rough edges with your fingers. When your sculpture dries, you can paint it.

Technique Tips

Aluminum Foil

Foil can be pinched and squeezed to make sculptures.

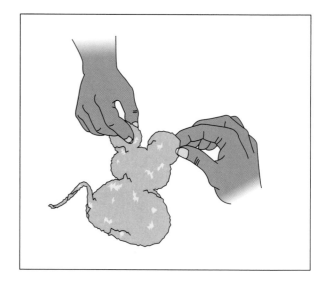

Building with Forms

To make sculptures with paper or cardboard forms, place the forms together and use masking tape to join them.

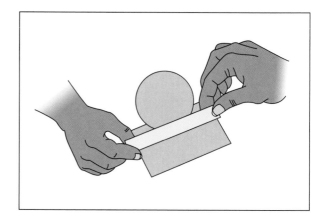

Technique Tips

Puppets

Cut out the pieces for your puppet from paper.

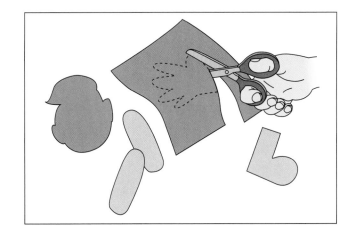

Use a hole punch to make holes at the joints where two pieces go together.

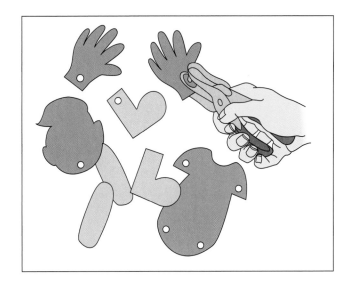

Use a brad to join the pieces. Stick a brad through both holes, and then unfold the metal clamps.

Technique Tips

Needlework

Thread your needle, or get help threading your needle. Tie a knot in the end of the thread.

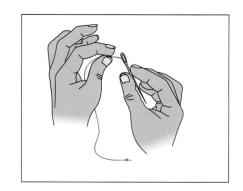

Carefully push the needle up from the bottom through the fabric where you want your stitch to start. Pull the needle through until the knot catches.

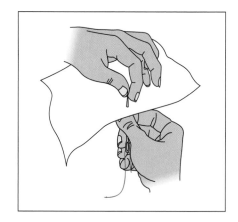

Carefully push the needle down through the fabric where you want your stitch to end. Repeat.

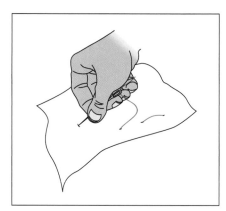

Technique Tips

Sewing a Book

1. Find the center of the fold and make a mark. Measure 1″ above and below the center mark.

2. Use a tapestry needle and poke holes through your marks.

3. Thread your needle and go through the top hole from the outside of your book and back through the center hole. Cut your thread so that you can tie both ends together.

4. Repeat for the bottom of your book.

Activity Tips

Expressive Lines

🎨 Creative Expression

1. Think about the different kinds of weather where you live. What mood does each create?

2. Select the type of weather condition you would like to draw. Make a rough sketch to plan the scene. Experiment with different kinds of lines. Decide which lines will best express the mood you wish to create.

3. Draw your scene. Be sure to use the right kinds of lines to create a calm or active feeling.

Line Variations

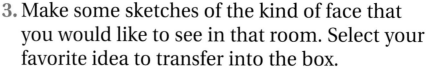

🎨 Creative Expression

1. Think about a room you would like to decorate. Is it your classroom, your bedroom, or some other room?

2. Draw the room showing the floor, walls, and furniture, inside a shoebox.

3. Make some sketches of the kind of face that you would like to see in that room. Select your favorite idea to transfer into the box.

4. Using a variety of lines, draw the face in the box. Use black markers to complete the drawing.

Activity Tips

Shapes

🎨 Creative Expression

1. Arrange five objects of different shapes and sizes in a variety of ways. Select the best arrangement.

2. Which object captures your attention most? Outline the shape of that object on your paper. In the same way, add the shapes of the other objects.

3. Begin to fill your shapes with different colors. Use one color at a time in several places on your picture. Continue to do this until your paper is filled with color.

Complex Geometric Shapes

🎨 Creative Expression

1. Imagine a design you can create with complex geometric shapes.

2. Use your imagination to make a design using simple and complex geometric shapes.

3. Use your scrap paper to design a frame or border for your art.

Activity Tips

Shapes in Architecture

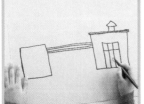

🎨 Creative Expression

1. Walk outside and choose an area of your school building that you would like to draw.

2. Point out all the geometric shapes you see. Then look for the free-form shapes.

3. Draw the area of the school building you selected. Make sure you include all the geometric and free-form shapes you see.

Shapes of People

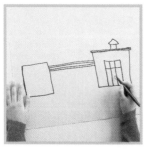

🎨 Creative Expression

1. Ask a classmate to be your model. Select some objects from the classroom to use as props. Have your model use these props as they pose for you.

2. Look carefully at your model. Find the geometric and free-form shapes.

3. Use chalk to draw your model and the props. Use lines to create the geometric and free-form shapes you see. Fill the shapes with oil pastels.

Activity Tips

Unit 2 · Lesson 1 **Positive and Negative Space**

🎨 Creative Expression

1. Study *Sleeveless Shirt* and *Tree of Life*.

2. Choose a light color, full-size sheet of construction paper. Choose a contrasting color for the half sheet.

3. Lay the half sheet on top of the left side of the full sheet of construction paper.

4. When all pieces are positioned in the correct location, glue them into place.

Unit 2 · Lesson 2 **Creating Depth**

🎨 Creative Expression

1. Think about a place where there are lots of animals.

2. Make a rough sketch of the animals and other objects you want in your scene. Show depth by drawing animals and objects larger in the foreground and smaller in the background.

3. Fill your scene with color.

Activity Tips

Overlapping

 **Creative Expression**

1. Think about the different parts of a tree. How do the branches look? Sketch some, using different kinds of lines.

2. Draw some trees, making each tree's branches and leaves overlap to create a feeling of depth.

3. Fill your page, and touch all edges of the paper with your lines and shapes.

Unit 2 · Lesson 4 **Form**

Creative Expression

1. Have you ever seen a sculpture shaped like an animal form?

2. Notice the sculptures *The Walking Flower* and *Sun God*. What are the similarities and differences?

3. Find objects outdoors to be used to create an animal.

4. Use a rectangular box or juice can for the body. Use pieces of cardboard for the legs. You can draw texture on your animal sculpture.

Activity Tips

Unit 2 · Lesson 5 — Relief Sculpture

Creative Expression

1. Describe what is happening in both of the relief works. Do some of the areas appear to stick out more than others?

2. If you could make a relief sculpture that told a story about you, what would you put on the relief?

3. Roll out a slab of clay and create a relief of objects or a picture of a person who is important to you.

4. With a pencil, draw the design into the clay. Press lightly so as not to cut through the clay.

Unit 2 · Lesson 6 — Three-Dimensional Art to Wear

 Creative Expression

1. Think about small objects that have interesting shapes.

2. Cut a piece of cardboard into a geometric shape. Arrange objects on top of the cardboard in different ways. Glue your favorite arrangement to the cardboard.

3. When dry, cover the surface with foil.

4. Punch a hole at the top of your design. Pass a piece of yarn or ribbon through the hole, and tie the ends to make a necklace.

Activity Tips

Looking at Color

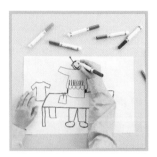

🎨 Creative Expression

1. Think of ways that you, your family, and friends celebrate special events. Choose one event for your drawing. What colors will you need to include? What colors will you use to show the mood of this event?

2. Draw the event or occasion with colored markers on white construction paper.

3. Fill your paper with color.

· ·

Intermediate Colors

🎨 Creative Expression

1. The colors must be in the correct order.

2. Use primary paint colors to mix secondary and intermediate colors.

3. The wheel does not have to be round, or even a circle.

4. Plan and decide on a way to indicate the difference between primary, secondary, and intermediate colors.

Activity Tips

Color Wheel

Creative Expression

1. Think about an amusement ride you can make using all the colors from a color wheel in order.

2. Be creative. Remember that the colors have to follow the order of the color wheel.

Cool Colors

Creative Expression

1. Think of ideas dealing with your environment, such as an animal habitat or a playground in the year 3001. Choose an idea and then sketch a few things you would find there.

2. Select several pieces of cool-colored paper. Choose one piece for the base. Outline objects you want in your environment on the other sheets of paper and cut them out. Add detail with oil pastels in cool colors. Attach the objects to your base.

Activity Tips

Warm Colors

🎨 Creative Expression

1. Use your imagination to create a fantasy landscape that includes three unrelated items such as a matchstick, a bowling pin, and a pair of sunglasses. Make a rough sketch of your idea.

2. Use lines to draw your idea on a sheet of white paper with warm-colored oil pastels.

3. Mix a variety of warm values with watercolor paint. Paint your scene. Remember that the values will get lighter as you add more water to your paint.

Unit 3 · Lesson 6 **Color Contrast**

🎨 Creative Expression

1. In a small group, make a list of underwater creatures. Draw the creatures on sheets of warm-colored construction paper. Use warm-colored oil pastels to add color and detail.

2. As a team, paint an underwater scene on a large sheet of paper. Mix cool colors to create water and plant life.

3. When the paint is dry, arrange and glue the sea creatures in place.

Activity Tips

Formal Balance

Creative Expression

1. Look at the artwork *Victorian Parlor II* by Horace Pippin. Think about how the outside of this house might look.

2. On a large piece of paper, draw the outside of the house. Use formal balance in your drawing.

3. Fill the house with color. Add trees and plants. Use formal balance in your landscape too.

Formal Balance in Masks

Creative Expression

1. Think of how you want to use your mask and what it will express. Make a few sketches until you get one you like.

2. Look at your sketch. Then cut pieces of cardboard tubes and boxes to form the features. Tape or glue them in place onto your base. Balance some of the forms formally.

3. Dip torn strips of newspaper into paste. Apply them to the mask.

Activity Tips

Symmetry

Creative Expression

1. Think of a real or imaginary creature. Make several sketches.
2. Fold a sheet of paper in half. The fold will be your central axis.
3. Using small pieces of colored paper, cut out shapes to represent features such as eyes. Using symmetry, place these features on your totem. Glue the pieces into place.
4. Use symmetry to add other details.
5. Join the edges of your paper together to form a cylinder.

Approximate Symmetry

Creative Expression

1. Look at your face in the mirror. Notice how it is almost exactly the same on both sides.
2. Use approximate symmetry to draw a self-portrait.
3. In the spaces around your portrait, draw objects that are important to you.
4. Add color.

Activity Tips

Visual Texture

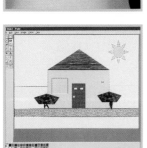

Creative Expression

1. Make a few quick sketches to show what your house looks like. Include things around your house like sidewalks or bushes.

2. Now use the draw tool to draw a picture of your house and the area around it. Think about the textures that are visible, like bricks.

3. Use the fill and texture tools to add color and texture to the drawing.

• •

Unit 4 · Lesson 6 **Tactile Texture**

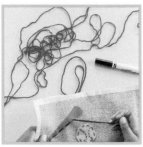

Creative Expression

1. Think about symbols that represent you. Make several sketches.

2. Choose your best sketch as a model. Cut out shapes from colorful fabric. Arrange them on a piece of burlap.

3. Attach shapes using glue. Stitch around the edges of each shape and add details with a marker.

Activity Tips

Pattern and Motif

🎨 Creative Expression

1. First, cut your potato in half. On the cut side, use the pointed side of a pencil to make a design in the potato.

2. Dip the cut side of the potato in paint.

3. Randomly press the potato onto newspaper or a brown paper bag to create a pattern.

4. Use the paper as wrapping paper for a gift.

Regular Patterns

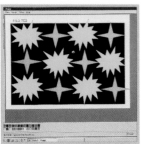

🎨 Creative Expression

1. Use the auto-shape tool to create a square.

2. Use the line and auto-shape tools to create a design in the square.

3. Use the fill tool to color in the design.

4. Select the whole design and copy.

5. Paste the design over several times, to create a regular pattern.

6. Enlarge the completed square design.

7. Print your work.

Activity Tips

Alternating Patterns

Creative Expression

1. Create two motifs that you would wear on a shirt or jacket, such as cars, books, bicycles, or footballs.

2. Draw the article of clothing. Use an alternating pattern of the two motifs you created.

3. Color with crayons.

Rhythm

Creative Expression

1. Make three to five pinch pots. The smallest should have a 3″ opening.

2. Use scoring and slip to join the pots at their sides to make an interesting rhythm of round pots.

3. Smooth the places where they are joined using a clay tool or your fingers.

4. Decorate your bowls by pressing in or adding on patterns using clay tools or found objects.

Activity Tips

Visual Rhythm

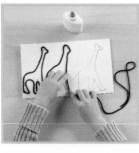

 Creative Expression

1. Think about things you like to see in a parade. Do you like floats, marching bands, clowns, horses, elephants, or antique cars?

2. Make sketches of things you want in your parade. Draw yourself as the grand marshal or leader of the parade.

3. Select your best sketches and use chalk to transfer them to large paper.

4. Paint your parade.

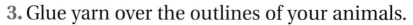

Three-Dimensional Rhythm

 Creative Expression

1. Think about an animal you would like to use. Look at pictures of that animal.

2. Make sketches of the animal. Select your best sketches and draw the animal several times on the cardboard to create a rhythmic repetition of the animal.

3. Glue yarn over the outlines of your animals.

4. Cover the surface with aluminum foil. Start pressing foil near the center. As you work, gently press the foil around each raised line with your fingertips.

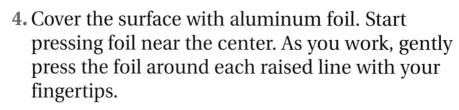

Activity Tips

Harmony

Creative Expression

1. Begin by making a pinch pot. Then roll a coil to make arms that will fit halfway around the rim of your pot. Roll a sphere to make a head.

2. Using proper joining techniques, attach the arms and head to the rim of your pot. Add clay for hair. With your clay tools add details such as hands, eyes, and a mouth. Add texture to the hair.

3. Choose related colors to paint or glaze your figural pot once it has been fired.

Variety

Creative Expression

1. Think about how you will use your weaving. Select a variety of ribbons, natural fibers, and yarn for your weaving.

2. Cut out a piece of cardboard, and notch it on the top and the bottom. Then string the warp thread on it.

3. Weave your fibers to create variety.

Activity Tips

Emphasis

Creative Expression

1. Use the ellipse tool to draw a circle. Use the draw tool to draw something from nature within the circle.

2. Use the line tool to draw diagonal lines that connect to the circle. Use the fill tool to fill the sections around the circle with shades of gray.

3. Use the brush tool to paint the design inside the circle. Make it colorful.

Emphasis Through Decoration

Creative Expression

1. Use a sheet of paper for the cover. Wet the paper with water. Use a wash of warm or cool colors. Let it dry.

2. On a sheet of construction paper, recreate your drawing from the Practice activity. Cut the image out. Glue a paper ring to the back.

3. Stack three sheets of paper on top of your cover. Fold it in half so that the cover is on the outside. Stitch your pages together. Glue the paper ring to the cover so the image is raised from the surface.

Activity Tips

Unity Through Color

🎨 Creative Expression

1. Flatten a palm-sized ball of clay until it is about as thick as your little finger. Fold the clay like a taco. Score the edges and seal it along the top.

2. Shape clay into fins and eyes. Attach by scoring, applying slip, and smoothing. Pinch a tail.

3. Use clay tools to create scales. Make interesting textures on your fish.

4. After the fish is fired, glaze or paint it with one color to unify all the texture and parts.

Unity, Repetition, and Grouping

🎨 Creative Expression

1. Think about insects and reptiles with interesting shapes. Use crayons to cover a sheet of paper with many different colors. Then paint the whole surface with thinned black ink until you can no longer see the color.

2. While the ink is drying, sketch a few real or imaginary reptiles and insects on scratch paper. Choose some to draw.

3. Engrave the creatures by scratching lines and line patterns in the black background with a paper clip. Add detail and texture.

Visual Index

Artist Unknown
Jar
2000–3000 B.C.
(page 186)

Artist Unknown
*Hunting Scene on Handle
from a large bowl*
2nd century. A.D. (page 83)

Artist Unknown
Portrait of a Boy
2nd century.
(page 138)

Artist Unknown
*Hat: Birds and
Geometric Patterns*
c. 700–1000.
(page 100)

Artist Unknown
*Presentation of Captives
to a Maya Ruler*
c. 785. (page 82)

Artist Unknown
Jar
12th century.
(page 127)

Artist Unknown
Cover of Armenian Book
13th century. (page 198)

Artist Unknown
Mihrab
1354. (page 49)

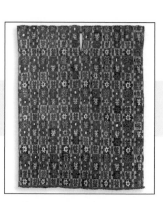

Artist Unknown
Tunic
15th–16th century.
(page 164)

Artist Unknown
Sleeveless Shirt
(Two Cats)
c. 1438–1532.
(page 66)

Artist Unknown
Covered Jar
c. 1522 –1566.
(page 117)

Mir Sayyid Ali
Nighttime in the Palace
c. 1539–1543. (page 180)

Giovanni Antonio Canal
The Clock Tower in the Piazza
San Marco
c. 1730. (page 53)

Caleb Gardner
Easy Chair
1758. (page 157)

Thomas Gainsborough
Jonathan Buttall: The
Blue Boy
c. 1770. (page 57)

Artist Unknown
Washington's Headquarters
1780
c. 1876. (page 70)

Artist Unknown
Mask with Seal or Sea
Otter Spirit
19th century. (page 131)

Artist Unknown
Senufo Face Mask
19th–20th century.
(page 130)

Joseph Mallord William Turner
Mortlake Terrace
1826. (page 71)

Artist Unknown
Thunderbird Shield
c. 1830. (page 147)

John James Audubon
Great Blue Heron
1834. (page 154)

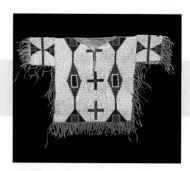

Rosa Bonheur
Ploughing in the Nivernais Region
1849. (page 168)

Artist Unknown
Child's Beaded Shirt
c. 1865. (page 190)

Artist Unknown
Double Saddlebag
1875. (page 48)

Gustave Caillebotte
Paris Street Rainy Day
1877. (page 142)

Edgar Degas
Little Dancer, Aged Fourteen
c. 1881. (page 64)

Claude Monet
Japanese Bridge over a Pool of Water Lilies
1899. (page 36)

Lundin Kudo
Gin Matsuba
20th century.
(page 203)

Artist Unknown
Necklace
20th century.
(page 86)

Artist Unknown
Symmetrical View of a Totem Pole
20th century. (page 134)

Artist Unknown
Cote d'Ivoire
1900. (page 87)

Frederic Remington
Mountain Man
1903. (page 184)

Artist Unknown
Collar
c. 1900–1925. (page 165)

John Sloan
Hairdresser's Window
1907. (page 194)

Henri Rousseau
The Football Players
1908. (page 150)

Wassily Kandinsky
Improvisation No. 27
1912. (page 40)

Allen E. Cole
Silas Johnson
1920s. (page 56)

Arthur Lismer
September Gale,
Georgian Bay
1921. (page 37)

Pablo Picasso
Mother and Child
1922. (page 34)

Georgia O'Keeffe
Red Canna
1925-1928. (page 113)

Edward Hopper
The City
1927. (page 52)

Diego Rivera
Kneeling Child on Yellow
Background
1927. (page 94)

Paul Klee
Rotes Haus
1929. (page 112)

Vaclav Vytlacil
Composition
1931. (page 45)

Shirley Ximena Hopper Russell
Boy's Day
1935. (page 96)

Henri Matisse
Women in Blue
1937. (page 207)

Man Ray
La Fortune
1938. (page 104)

Horace Pippin
Victorian Parlor II
1945. (page 126)

Fred Kabotie
Pueblo Scene Corn Dance, Hopi
1947. (page 173)

Philip Evergood
Her World
1948. (page 139)

Calvin Jones
Brilliant as the Sun upon the World
c. 1950 (page 105)

Fernand Leger
The Walking Flower
1951. (page 78)

Milton Avery
Sea Grasses and Blue Sea
1958. (page 109)

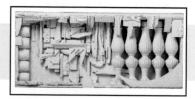

Louise Nevelson
Case with Five Balusters
1959. (page 177)

Jacob Lawrence
Parade
1960. (page 172)

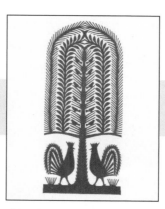

Stanistawa Bakula
Tree of Life
1962. (page 67)

René Magritte
Carte Blanche (The Blank Signature)
1965. (page 90)

Ayako Miyawaki
Various Fish
1967. (page 146)

Andy Warhol
Flowers
1967. (page 202)

Richard Estes
Diner
1971. (page 143)

Joseph Jean-Gilles
Haitian Landscape
1973. (page 75)

Audrey Flack
Strawberry Tart
Supreme
1974. (page 124)

Jacob Lawrence
Builders No. 1
1971. (page 60)

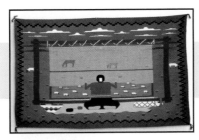

Isabel John
Pictorial Tapestry
1980s. (page 191)

Aurelio and
Francisco Flores
Candelabra
c. 1980. (page 135)

Jonathan Borofsky
Self Portrait with Big Ears
Learning to Be Free
1980–1984. (page 41)

Nancy Youngblood
Pottery Vessels
1980–1985. (page 187)

Al Held
Piero's Piazza
1982. (page 97)

Niki de Saint Phalle
Sun God
1983. (page 79)

William T. Wiley
Remedial
Archaeology and
the Like
1986. (page 101)

Wayne Thiebaud
Lighted City
1987. (page 108)

Dorothy Djukulul
Warrnyu (Flying Foxes)
1989. (page 161)

Wayne Thiebaud
Display Rows
1989. (page 120)

Idelle Weber
Pistia Kew
1989. (page 116)

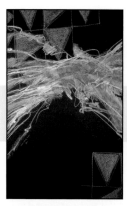

Willis Bing Davis
Ancestral Spirit
Dance
1990. (page 206)

Sylvia Plimack Mangold
The Locust Trees with
Maple
1990. (page 75)

Faith Ringgold
The Sunflower Quilting Bee at Arles
1991. (page 210)

Philip Moulthrop
White Pine Mosaic
1993. (page 156)

Tom Loeser
Four by Four
1994. (page 160)

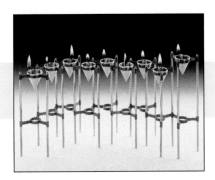

Abrasha
Hannukkah Menorah
1995. (page 169)

Janet Fish
Yellow Pad
1997. (page 44)

Pamela Spitzmueller
British Museum Memoir
1997. (page 199)

John Hoover
Looner Eclipse
1999. (page 176)

Robert Cottingham
Jane's Remington
2000. (page 195)

Glossary

Pronunciation Key: at; lāte; câre; fäther; set; mē; it; kīte; ox rōse; ô in bought; coin; book; tōo; form; out; up; ūse; tûrn; ə sound in about, chicken, pencil, cannon, circus, chair; hw in which; ring; shop; thin; there; zh in treasure.

A

alternating pattern (ôl' tər nāt ing pat' ərn), *noun*   A pattern in which one motif is repeated after a second, different motif

appliqué (ap' li kā), *noun*   An art form in which cutout fabrics are attached to a larger surface

approximate symmetry (ə 'präk sə mət sim' i trē), *noun*   A special kind of formal balance where both sides of a design are almost exactly the same. One example is the human face: each side is almost the same as the other.

architect (är' kə tekt), *noun*   The artist who plans and designs buildings

architecture (är' kə tek' chər), *noun*   The art of designing and planning buildings

C

central axis (sen' trəl ak' sis), *noun*   An imaginary dividing line

color spectrum (kul' ər spek' trum), *noun*   The range of colors that comes from light. Rainbows are the most famous display of this spectrum in nature.

color wheel (kul' ər 'wēl), *noun*   The spectrum that artists use bent into the shape of a circle

complex geometric shapes (kom' pleks jē' ə met' rik shāps), *noun*   Shapes made by combining simple geometric shapes such as triangles, squares, and rectangles. Some examples of complex geometric shapes are diamonds, pentagons, trapezoids, hexagons, parallelograms, and octagons.

contrast (kon' trast), *noun*   Showing differences between things

cool colors (kül kul' erz), *noun*
Blue, green, and violet. These are
colors that remind us of cool
objects like grass, water, and ice.
These colors can create a sense of
depth because they seem to move
away from the viewer.

culture (kəl chər), *noun*
Another word for *custom*

curved (kûrvd), *adj.* Lines that
bend and change direction slowly.
They give a feeling of graceful
movement.

D

depth (depth), *noun* 1. The
appearance of distance; 2. How
far something extends toward or
away from the viewer

diagonal (dī ag' ə nəl), *noun (adj.)*
Lines that are slanted. They look
as if they are falling or rising. They
make things look active.

E

emphasis (em' fə sis), *noun* The
way an artist makes something in
a work of art stand out

exaggerate (eg zaj' ə rā' te), *verb*
To make much larger than actual
size

F

formal balance (fôr' mel bal' əns),
noun Organization of elements
where equal objects are on
opposite sides of the artwork

forms (formz), *noun* Three-
dimensional objects that can be
measured in three ways: height,
width, and depth. Some examples
of simple forms are spheres,
cones, pyramids, and cylinders.

free-form shapes (frē' fôrm'
shāps), *noun* Uneven and
irregular shapes. Puddles, clouds,
and flowers are examples of free-
form shapes found in nature.

freestanding forms (frē stan' ding
formz), *noun* Forms that can be
seen from all around

G

geometric shapes (je' ə met' rik
shāps), *noun* A math shape such
as a circle, triangle, or rectangle
that is usually found in objects
that are made by people.
Buildings, furniture, and road
signs are some examples of
geometric shapes.

H

harmony (här' mə nē), *noun* The peaceful look made when related elements of art are put together. Artists create harmony by repeating lines, colors, shapes, textures, and objects.

highlight (hī līt'), *noun* Small areas of white used to show the brightest spots on an object

horizontal (hôr' ə zon təl), *adj.* Lines that move straight across from side to side. They give a feeling of calm peace.

hue (hū), *noun* Another word for color

I

interior designers (in tîr' ē ər di zī' nər), *noun* Artists who decorate the inside of a building

intermediate colors (in' tər mē' dē it kul' ərs), *noun* Colors made by mixing a primary color and a secondary color. There are six intermediate colors—red-orange, yellow-orange, yellow-green, blue-green, blue-violet, and red-violet.

J

jeweler (jü' ə lər), *noun* An artist who designs and makes jewelry

jewelry (jü' əl rē), *noun* Three-dimensional artwork that is made for people to wear

L

lines (līnz), *noun* Marks drawn by a tool such as a pencil, pen, or paintbrush as it moves across a surface

line variety (līn və rī' ə tē), *noun* The different possibilities in the character of lines. For example, lines can be long or short, thick or thin, rough or smooth, and broken or solid.

M

mask (mask), *noun* A three-dimensional art form of sculpted faces

motif (mō tēf), *noun* The unit of repetition in the pattern. The motif is made of objects or art elements.

N

negative space (neg' ə tiv spas'), *noun* Empty space in an artwork

O

overlapping (o' vər lap ing), *verb* One object covers part of another object. Overlapping makes the object in front seem closer to the viewer.

P

pattern (pat' ərn), *noun* A repeated surface decoration

positive space (poz' i tiv spas'), *noun* The area that shapes and objects fill

primary colors (pri' mer ē kul' erz), *noun* Red, yellow, and blue. They cannot be made by mixing colors.

R

random pattern (ran' dəm pat' ərn), *noun* A pattern in which the motif is repeated in no particular order

regular pattern (reg' yə lər pat' ərn), *noun* A pattern in which the motif is repeated in an even manner

relief sculptures (ri lēf' skulp' chər), *noun* Forms that stand out from a flat surface, like coins

repetition (rep' i tish' ən), *noun* Lines, shapes, colors, or textures that are repeated throughout an artwork

rest (rest), *noun* The negative space between repetitions of the motif

rhythm (rith' əm), *noun* A feeling created by the repetition of a positive shape or form. That object is the beat. The negative space between the repetitions is the rest.

S

sculpture (skulp' chər), *noun* Three-dimensional art

secondary colors (sek' ən der' ē kul' erz), *noun* Orange, green, and violet. These colors are made by mixing two primary colors.

shade (shād), *noun* Darker values of a color

shape (shāp) *noun* Flat, two-dimensional areas that are geometric or free-form. They can be measured in only two ways: height and width.

spectral colors (spek' trəl kul' ər) *noun* The colors of the light spectrum: red, orange, yellow, green, blue, and violet

symmetry (sim' i trē), *noun* Two halves of a design are identical, mirror images of each other. The two halves are divided by the central axis. Everything on one side of the central axis is balanced by the objects on the other side.

T

tactile texture (tak' təl teks' chər), *noun* Texture that can be felt

three-dimensional rhythm (thrē di men' shə nəl rith' əm), *noun* A principle of design that indicates movement by the repetition of elements in a form

tint (tint), *noun* Lighter values of a color

two-dimensional (tü' di men' shə nəl), *adj.* flat and can be measured by length and width

U

unity (ū' ni tē), *noun* The feeling of wholeness in a work of art. Artists use repetition and grouping to show that different parts of a work belong together.

V

value (val' ū), *noun* The lightness or darkness of a color.

variety (və ri' ə tē), *noun* Different lines, shapes, colors, and textures to make a work of art interesting.

vertical lines (vür tə kəl līnz), *noun* Lines that move straight up and down. They make things look tall, steady, and calm.

visual rhythm (vizh' ü əl rith' əm), *noun* The feeling of movement created when artists repeat colors, shapes, lines, and textures to lead the viewer's eyes through a work of art

visual texture (vizh' ü əl teks' chər), *noun* Texture that you see

W

warm colors (wōrm' kul' ərz),
noun   Yellow, orange, and red.
These colors remind the viewer of
a sense of warmth in a work of
art. These colors often are the first
to attract the viewer's attention.

Z

zigzag (zig' zag) *noun (adj.)*
Diagonal lines that connect. They
give a feeling of excitement.

Index

Photo Credits

Cover National Gallery of Art, Washington, D.C. Collection of Mr. and Mrs. Paul Mellon, Image © 2003 Board of Trustees, National Gallery of Art, Washington. © 2004 C. Herscovici, Brussels/Artists Rights Society (ARS), New York; 5 The Baltimore Museum of Art: The Cone Collection formed by Dr. Claribel Cone and Miss Etta Cone of Baltimore, Maryland. © 2004 Estate of Pablo Picasso/Artists Rights Society (ARS), New York; 6 (c) The Metropolitan Museum of Art, H.O. Havemeyer Collection, Bequest of Mrs. H.O. Havemeyer, 1929. Photograph © The Metropolitan Museum of Art; 07 San Francisco Museum of Modern Art, Bequest of Elise S. Hass. Photo by Ben Blackwell; 8 © Allen Memorial Art Museum, Oberlin College, National Endowment for the Arts Museum Purchase Plan and Fund for Contemporary Art 1974; 9 Collection of the Orlando Museum of Art, Gift of Council of 101 and Mr. and Mrs. William duPont, III; 10 The Carleton Collection; 12 (tl) Collection of Whitney Museum of American Art, New York. Photography Copyright © 1998: Whitney Museum of American Art, New York, (tr) The Baltimore Museum of Art: The Cone Collection formed by Dr. Claribel Cone and Miss Etta Cone of Baltimore, Maryland. © 2004 Estate of Pablo Picasso/Artists Rights Society (ARS), New York; (bl) Home and Away Gallery; 13 (tl) National Museum of Women in the Arts. Gift of Wallace and Wilhelmina Holladay, (tr) Schmidt Bingham Gallery. New York, New York., (bl) Photography by Ansel Adams. Used with permission of the Trustees of the Ansel Adams Publishing Rights Trust. All Rights Reserved. © Digital Image © The Museum of Modern Art/Licensed by SCALA/Art Resource, NY, (br) The Metropolitan Museum of Art, the Michael C. Rockefeller Collection, Purchase, Nelson A. Rockefeller Gift, 1964. (1978.412.489) Photograph by Schecter Lee. Photograph © 1986 The Metropolitan Museum of Art; 15 (tl) Photograph Oliver Folk Art, (bl) © Digital Image © The Museum of Modern Art/Licensed by SCALA/Art Resource, NY. © Henry Moore Foundation, (br) The Metropolitan Museum of Art, Gift of Mrs. J. Insley Blair, 1950. Photograph © 1981 The Metropolitan Museum of Art; 16 Image © The Museum of Modern Art/Licensed by SCALA/Art Resource, NY; 17 The Metropolitan Museum of Art, H.O. Havemeyer Collection, Bequest of Mrs. H.O. Havemeyer, 1929. (29.100.113) Photograph © 1996 The Metropolitan Museum of Art; 18 © Jacob and Gwendolyn Lawrence Foundation. Photograph Courtesy of Gwendolyn Knight Lawrence/Art Resource, NY; 19 Collection of The Newark Museum, Newark, New Jersey. Purchased 1937 Felix Fund Bequest Fund; 20 San Francisco Museum of Modern Art, Bequest of Elise S. Hass. Photo by Ben Blackwell; 21 The Metropolitan Museum of Art, New York, New York; 22 (t, tcl, tcr, br, bcr) © Photodisc/Getty Images, Inc, (bcl, bl) © Digital Vision/Getty Images, Inc; 23 (t) © Corbis, (tcl, tcr, bl, bcl, bc) © Photodisc/Getty Images, Inc, (br) © Index Stock; 24, 26, 28, 30 The Metropolitan Museum of Art, Arthur Hoppock Hearn Fund, 1958. (58.26) Photograph © 1992 The Metropolitan Museum of Art; 32-33 © Aaron Haupt; 34 The Baltimore Museum of Art: The Cone Collection formed by Dr. Claribel Cone and Miss Etta Cone of Baltimore, Maryland. © 2004 Estate of Pablo Picasso/Artists Rights Society (ARS), New York; 35 © Bettmann/Corbis; 36 The Metropolitan Museum of Art, H.O. Havemeyer Collection, Bequest of Mrs. H.O. Havemeyer, 1929. (29.100.113) Photograph © 1996 The Metropolitan Museum of Art; 37 © National Gallery of Canada. Purchased 1926; 38 © Eclipse Studios; 39 Frank Fortune; 40 The Metropolitan Museum of Art, The Alfred Stieglitz Collection, 1949. (49.70.1). Photograph © 1987 The Metropolitan Museum of Art. © 2004 Artists Rights Society (ARS), New York/ADAGP, Paris; 41 Collection of the Modern Art Museum of Fort Worth, Museum Purchase; 42 © Eclipse Studios; 43 Randy Ellett; 44 Collection of the Columbus Museum, Columbus, GA; Museum purchase made possible by Norman S. Rothschild in honor of his parents Aleen and Irwin B. Rothschild. © Janet Fish/Licensed by VAGA, New York, NY; 45 Norton Museum of Art, West Palm Beach, Florida, Gift of the Estate of Vaclav Vytlacil, 99.104; 46 © Eclipse Studios; 47 Randy Ellett; 48 Detroit Institute of Arts, Detroit, Michigan; 49 The Metropolitan Museum of Art, Harris Brisbane Dick Fund, 1939. (39.20) Photograph © 1982 The Metropolitan Museum of Art; 50 © Eclipse Studios; 51 Photo by Ko Yoshida; 52 Collection of The University of Arizona Museum of Art, Tucson, Gift of C. Leonard Pfeiffer x45.9.23; 53 The Nelson-Atkins Museum of Art, Kansas City, Missouri (Gift of Byron and Eileen Cohen) F85-17/1 A-D photograph by Mel McLean; 54 (tl) Jodi Cobb/National Geographic Society/Getty Images, Inc, (tcl) Digital Vision/Getty Images, Inc, (tcr, bl, bcl, bcr) Photodisc/Getty Images, Inc, (tr) Michael Melford/The Image Bank/Getty Images, Inc, (b) © Eclipse Studios, (br) Alfredo Maiquez/Lonely Planet Images/Getty Images, Inc; 55 Frank Fortune; 56 Western Reserve Historical Society; 57 © SuperStock; 58 (tl) Digital Vision/Getty Images, Inc, (tr, cr) Photodisc/Getty Images, Inc, (b) © Eclipse Studios, (cl) SRA photo, (cr) Photodisc/Getty Images, Inc; 59 Frank Fortune; 60 © Jacob and Gwendolyn Lawrence Foundation; 62 Taxi/Getty Images, Inc; 63 Don Perdue; 64 The Metropolitan Museum of Art, H.O. Havemeyer Collection, Bequest of Mrs. H.O. Havemeyer, 1929. Photograph © The Metropolitan Museum of Art; 65 © Francis G. Mayer/Corbis; 66 The Metropolitan Museum of Art, The Michael C. Rockefeller Memorial Collection, Bequest of Nelson A. Rockefeller, 1979. (1979.206.1131) Photograph © 1981 The Metropolitan Museum of Art; 67 From the Girard Foundation Collection, in the Museum of International Folk Art, a unit of the Museum of New Mexico, Santa Fe, New Mexico; 68 © Eclipse Studios; 69 Randy Ellett; 70 Smithsonian American Art Museum/Art Resource, NY; 71 National Gallery of Art, Washington, DC. Andrew W. Mellon Collection, Image © 2003 Board of Trustees, National Gallery of Art, Washington; 72 © Eclipse Studios; 73 Randy Ellett; 74 Brooke Alexander Gallery; 75 Collections of the Art Museum of the Americas - Organization of American States; 76 © Eclipse Studios; 77 Randy Ellett; 78 Albright-Knox Art Gallery. © 2004 Artists Rights Society (ARS), New York/ADAGP, Paris; 79 Photograph © Becky Cohen. © 2004 Artists Rights Society (ARS), New York; 80 © Eclipse Studios; 81 Randy Ellett; 82 Copyright © 2003 Kimbell Art Museum; 83 The Metropolitan Museum of Art, Fletcher Fund, 1934 (34.33) Photograph © 1995 The Metropolitan Museum of Art; 84 © Eclipse Studios; 85 Randy Ellett; 87 Museum of Fine Arts, Houston, Texas. Photograph The Bridgeman Art Library; 88 (t) ThinkStock LLC/Index Stock Imagery, (b) © Eclipse Studios; 89 Randy Ellett; 90 National Gallery of Art, Washington, D.C. Collection of Mr. and Mrs. Paul Mellon, Image © 2003 Board of Trustees, National Gallery of Art, Washington. © 2004 C. Herscovici, Brussels/Artists Rights Society (ARS), New York; 92 © Andreas Pollok/Getty Images, Inc; 93 Craig Schwartz © 1998; 94 San Francisco Museum of Modern Art, Bequest of Elise S. Hass. Photo by Ben Blackwell; 95 © Corbis; 96 Honolulu Academy of Art; 97 Albright-